CW00469027

The Forest and Chase of
MALVERN

The Forest and Chase of
MALVERN

Pamela Hurle

Phillimore

2007

Published by
PHILLIMORE & CO. LTD
Shopwyke Manor Barn, Chichester, West Sussex, England
www.phillimore.co.uk

ISBN 978-1-86077-440-9

Printed and bound in Great Britain

Contents

List of Illustrations

Illustrations from the following sources are cordially acknowledged: David
Armitage, 92; Keith Wilson, 42; Malvern Hills Conservators, 17, 18, 51, 52, 75,
77, 78, 79, 80, 81, 82, 83, 84, 85, 86, 87, 88, 89, 90, 91, 93, 94, 95, 96, 97, 98
and 99; Peter Garner, frontispiece, 100; The Society of Antiquaries of London,
39; Mrs T.M. Berington and Worcestershire Record Office, 40; Worcestershire
Record Office and County Library, 20, 23, 37, 38, 46, 47 and 62.

Introduction

Malvern gave its name to one of the royal forests that William the Conqueror established soon after his Conquest of England in 1066. Called *Malferna* in Domesday Book, the area had been a hunting ground for pre-Conquest bishops for an unknown period. Since the seat of administration for William's royal forest was Potters Hanley (later Hanley Castle), it is perhaps surprising that the king did not call it Hanley Forest, particularly since he kept Hanley as one of his own manors. That name, however, has never been applied to it, so Malvern Forest (or Malvern Chase when hunting rights were granted to a subject) it remains.

My interest in Malvern Chase began over 30 years ago, when I first started to research and write about the history of several of its constituent parishes, promising myself that one day I would write a history of the Chase. This is it – my attempt to provide a realistic portrait of the Chase, making key documents more accessible and using a variety of illustrations, many of which have been hidden away for years. I hope that they will give as much pleasure to readers as their discovery has given to me.

The first chapters seek to explain the early history of the area and the impact on it of forest law, looking at medieval life in some of the settlements, and the limitations placed upon forest clearance and development. The middle chapters show that implementation of forest law was haphazard by the 16th century, and that in the 17th century Charles I's financial problems and his consequent disafforestation freed inhabitants from forest restrictions.

Although forest law ceased to apply here in the 17th century, it had affected life in many parishes for five and a half centuries, and its legacy can still be seen in this beautiful part of England so often called Malvern Country. Despite promises made in the disafforestation decree, the open spaces and commons were quite seriously eroded in the 18th and 19th centuries. The final chapters of this book are devoted to the attempts in the last century or so to protect the remains of Malvern Chase from the dangers of encroachment, enclosure, quarrying and that most damaging of all creatures – the human being. These last chapters pay particular attention to the role of two bodies charged with this protection – the Malvern Hills Conservators, who have since 1884 been guardians of a substantial portion of the lands of the medieval Chase, and the officers of the Area of Outstanding Natural Beauty set up after the Second World War.

Acknowledgements

This book has been particularly enhanced by maps which have never been published before. I wish to thank the Society of Antiquaries of London for permission to include the 1628 map – the earliest detailed map of Malvern Chase to have been discovered. I also wish to thank Mrs T.M. Berington and Robin Whittaker, Archives Manager at Worcester County Record Office, for permission to use the 1633 map preserved there in the Berington archives. I also thank the Malvern Hills Conservators for permission to use John Doharty's 1744 maps of the manor of Malvern, now owned by the Conservators, whose generosity further extended to allowing me to plunder their archives for illustrations. I am grateful to Ray Roberts, Valerie Goodbury and Robert Havard, who freely gave time and expertise to help me access this material.

The work of John France at Worcestershire Record Office has ensured a high standard of reproduction not only of the Malvern maps held there but also of copies of some of Maria Martin's drawings in the Buckle Collection, deposited in Worcester Library by Mrs Martin Buckle in the late 1930s with the intention of making them available to a wider public. I wish to thank staff at Norfolk Record Office for their help in trying to trace the current owner of this collection. I thank staff at Worcestershire Record Office and Worcester County Library for their help and for permission to publish the pictures.

I owe particular debts of gratitude to three people based at the Manor House in Malvern. They are Ian Rowat, Director of the Malvern Hills Conservators, Valerie Moore, the Conservators' Administrative Officer, and David Armitage of the A.O.N.B. office. They all kindly agreed to read my text, giving me not only the benefit of their considerable knowledge to effect improvement but also suggesting and providing illustrations relevant to points I wanted to make. I also thank Paul Esrich of the A.O.N.B. office and all the staff at the Manor House, who have always been so helpful and welcoming.

I am grateful to Mrs Rosemary Ballard, who kindly permitted me to read her late husband's archive on his grandfather, Stephen Ballard, and to quote from this source, and to my brother, Keith Wilson, for comment on my text.

My main sources are listed in the bibliography. Wherever possible I have acknowledged individual writers and artists, but some are long dead and now unknown. To all of them I express thanks for their work: it not only continues to give pleasure but also records, in words or pictures, information which would otherwise have been lost.

No historian can work in isolation, and I have been very fortunate in the support and encouragement I have received from many well-wishers. No-one has done more to encourage me in local history research and publication than my husband, whom I thank for over forty years of practical help and support. This has included reading the (almost) final text of each of my books, fulfilling the vital but extremely difficult role of critical friend – a task he has performed with remarkable tact and perseverance. Any errors, however, are my own.

Pamela Hurle
October 2006

Malvern Landscape
and Early History

Celia Fiennes, who travelled through this area in the 1690s, conjured up a delightful picture of the Malverns – 'they are at least 2 or 3 miles up and are in a Pirramidy fashion on the top'. A few years later she made a different comparison – they 'are like the Alps, and have much wet, the roads deep and difficult.'*

Neither pyramids nor Alps, the Malverns, which are granitic and extremely hard, have their origin in tectonic plate movements over 500 million years ago. The eight-mile range contains igneous rocks, formed as molten matter solidified. About 270 million years ago this igneous rock was forced to the surface. Later geological changes deposited other kinds of materials, such as limestone, shale and sandstone, the variety of such deposits making the hills of particular interest to geologists, whose researches continue. Lying underwater for about 160 million years, they have been above water and subject to erosion for the last 60 million

---

* Christopher Morris (ed.) *The Journeys of Celia Fiennes*, 1947, pp.43 and 336-7.

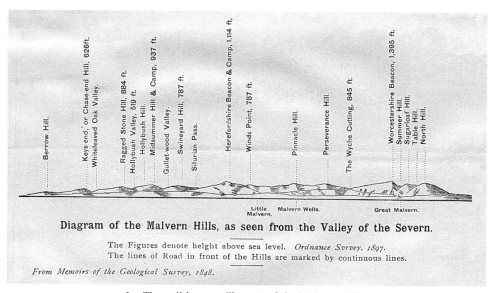

Diagram of the Malvern Hills, as seen from the Valley of the Severn.

The Figures denote height above sea level. *Ordnance Survey, 1897.*
The lines of Road in front of the Hills are marked by continuous lines.

From Memoirs of the Geological Survey, 1848.

1   *The well-known silhouette of the Malvern Hills.*

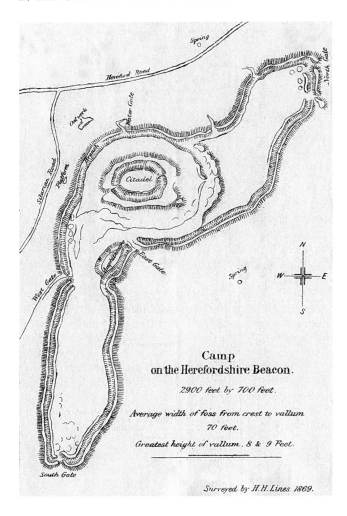

Camp
on the Herefordshire Beacon.

2900 feet by 700 feet.

Average width of foss from crest to vallum
70 feet.

Greatest height of vallum, 8 & 9 Feet.

Surveyed by H.H.Lines 1869.

2 *The Herefordshire Beacon was last excavated towards the end of the 19th century, when numerous historians and antiquarians worked on it enthusiastically. H.H. Lines was one of them, and produced plans and sketches of the ancient camps on the Herefordshire Beacon and on Midsummer Hill. His 1869 diagram marks the central citadel on the Herefordshire Beacon and the gates into the encampment.*

years.[*] They rise steeply, especially on the eastern side, running in a straight north-south line from North Hill to Chase End Hill at the southern end. The Malverns are usually assumed to have taken their name from ancient British or Welsh words (*moel* and *bryn*) meaning 'bare hill'.[†]

The Worcestershire Beacon at 1,395 feet is the highest point but probably the skyline of the Herefordshire Beacon at 1,114 feet is most impressive because of the ramparts and terraces still standing proud, more than 2,000 years after Iron-Age settlers made such astonishing communal effort to construct them. This superb example of an Iron-Age fort has survived extremes of climate through all these centuries and today faces the ravages of an additional, even more relentless, challenge – the million or more walkers and tourists who come each year to enjoy the Malvern Hills.

---

[*] Dr John Payne, Lecture on the Geology of the Malverns, May 2006.
[†] A.Mawer and F.M.Stenton, *The Place-Names of Worcestershire*,1969, p.210.

Little can be said with certainty about anything which happened here before the Iron Age, though it seems likely that late Bronze-Age settlers started the great earthwork which was later to be called the Shire Ditch.* Its name derived from the fact that it eventually defined part of the boundary between Worcestershire and Herefordshire when the shires were established.

In pre-historic times various tribes settled in the island which the Romans were to name Britannia, the ancient tribe that settled in this midland region being the Dobunni. During the Iron Age, about 450 years before the Romans conquered Britain, two hill forts were built on the Malverns. The larger one on the Herefordshire Beacon is still known as British Camp and the smaller one is further south, on Midsummer Hill, obscured by woodland. These forts or camps were sited so as to give a commanding view eastward across the Severn Plain and westward towards the Welsh mountains, enabling their inhabitants to defend themselves against possible attack from either side. On British Camp, without an internal water supply, they could not have held out for long but this was presumably not perceived as a major problem in ancient Britain when attacks were short sharp forays rather than lengthy wars of attrition.

_____

* Mark Bowden, *The Malvern Hills, An Ancient Landscape*, 2005, p.17.

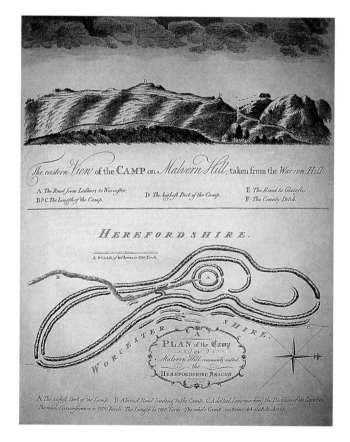

3 *This page from Dr Nash's* Worcestershire *shows late 18th-century perceptions of British Camp.*

Excavation in the late 19th century and, most particularly, that carried out in the 1960s on Midsummer Hill, has yielded much information about life in the Iron Age. The 1960s work was directed by Dr S.C. Stanford, whose very readable account contains the following advice, evocative in its knowledge of the hills:

> To appreciate truly the settlements of earlier peoples one should come to know them under all kinds of conditions. ... It is therefore appropriate that one should know the fatigue that comes at the end of the walk to the summit of the Herefordshire Beacon on a hot summer's day, and equally the biting cold of the east wind when it leaves thin traces of snow drifting in the lee of the ramparts. One should know the camps when the cloud has fallen upon them and visibility is down to a few yards; and one should know them too on those magic days of spring and autumn when the view is clear for miles around.*

Without benefit of modern earth-moving machinery, construction was obviously an immense community effort, the silhouette of British Camp still standing evidence of the builders' skill and determination in building over a mile of defences. Stanford portrayed a social organisation and discipline that involved men, women and even children, whose little hands could collect rock and stone together in wicker baskets. His suggestions of a total population of 1,500 to 2,000 on British Camp and 1,300 to 1,900 on Midsummer Hill have been questioned. A very large arable acreage as well as extensive pasturage would have been necessary to sustain so many people, and Stanford himself produced no conclusive evidence for such large communities.

After constructing the camps, these ancient communities, whatever their size, lived, according to Stanford, in small wood-framed huts, and farmed the surrounding countryside with wooden ploughs and iron sickles, grinding their corn with simple hand-mills. They obtained food and clothing from goats, pigs, cattle and sheep, which grazed more safely than their modern counterparts: fast-moving traffic on the roads dissecting the commons – remnants of ancient woodland – is now a serious hazard to animals roaming freely. The original track-ways

---

* S.C. Stanford, *The Malvern Hill Forts*, 1973, p.2.

4   *One of several 19th-century prints depicting the pass through the hills at the Wyche, where the cutting was widened in 1836. The stone was used to build the wall along the present main road into Malvern.*

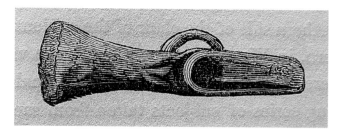

5 *A sketch, from Jabez Allies, of the bronze axe-head found in Malvern Link.*

used by early settlers cannot now be precisely located. Some led to Droitwich and its supplies of the vital salt that made it so important a town. Place-name origins are often controversial, and the belief that *wyche* was connected with salt has now been questioned. Nevertheless, although the date of the first cutting through the hills is not known, the Wyche cutting may have been a salt road from very early pre-historic times. Other tracks passed through the dense woods and more open scrub-land of settlements such as Castlemorton, Welland and Hanley to the River Severn – that important waterway with the potential to bring prosperity through trade or disaster through flood and disease.

A few prehistoric finds have been made, such as the bronze axe-head, weighing about 10 ounces and about 5½ inches long, found in Malvern Link. The 18th-century county historian, Dr Nash, reported this soon after its discovery. He also told of a much more exciting find a hundred years previously when in 1650 Thomas Taylor, digging a ditch round his cottage 'within the distance of a musket shot of the trenches' at British Camp, found a gold bracelet or coronet set with precious stones. He was probably delighted to get £37 for it from a Gloucester goldsmith, but the goldsmith did better, selling it for £250 to a London jeweller, who did best of all, breaking it up and selling the stones alone for £1,500. Attitudes to such finds were remarkably casual until quite recent times, and clearly we are unlikely to know the identity of the original owner of this treasure – perhaps a warrior chieftain of the tribe who built the camps. Gough's edition of Camden's *Britannia*, however, tells this story with the final price put at only £500 and gives an additional story of a coronet found in Colwall and sold for £150. His own warning is still appropriate, throwing doubt on all such tales:

> I fear this story is to be ranked with many others … and like those which the vulgar entertain of treasures to be found wherever there are remains of antiquity.[*]

Some stories are even more obviously false, but folklore preserves them as quaint relics of an age about which we know little. Clutter's Cave, for example, on the western side of the Herefordshire Beacon, is a man-made cave reputed to be the home of a giant (rather a small one to judge by the size of the cave and its entrance) who, angered by his wife's affair with another man, threw a huge stone at her. This landed in the centre of Colwall and is the origin of the Colwall Stone. A large stone outside the cave's entrance was said by Alfred Watkins and others to have been the door of the cave put to new use as an altar, on which human sacrifice took place.[†] More prosaically, Clutter's Cave may have been an 18th-century folly such as was common in country house estates, while Colwall

---

[*] Wm.Camden, *Britannia*, 1789, Vol. II, p.453.
[†] Alfred Watkins, *The Old Straight Track*, 1970, p.101.

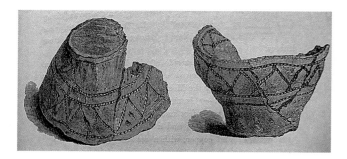

6   *A sketch, from Jabez Allies, of the little urn found at the top of the Worcestershire Beacon in 1849.*

Stone is seen simply as a conveniently placed mounting block to help riders to get on their horses. Jabez Allies* claimed that it was dragged by Francis Shuter and others with a team of oxen from a quarry in a copse at the Wyche in the 1770s. Watkins' theories on prehistoric tracks, ley lines and practices are now generally considered somewhat suspect, as is the folklore that Colwall took its name from the Latin *collis vallum* meaning hill trench. The name, rendered as *Colewelle* in Domesday Book, is much more likely to come from words meaning cool stream or spring.[†]

In 1910 the burial site of a large Bronze-Age settlement in Mathon, probably dating from the 10th century B.C., was found.[‡] This settlement was possibly connected with the discovery in 1849, by an Ordnance Survey team working on the Worcestershire Beacon, of part of a human skull. There was also a small decorated pottery urn, 2 ½ inches high, covering some cremated remains and, nearby, two lots of partially burnt human bones. Edwin Lees, who was a main inspiration of the Malvern and Worcestershire Naturalists' Clubs, procured these items from Private Harkin of the Ordnance Survey but, as with the Mathon site, there seems to have been no systematic excavation of the site. By 1983 the British Museum had custody only of 'an incense-cup ... found on the summit of the Worcestershire Beacon in 1849'.

In 1856 and 1857 two collections of rusty Iron-Age bars were found above the Wyche Road. Each about two feet long, they may have been the raw material from which implements were to have been made. It is, however, more likely that they were over 250 specimens of currency bars – the unwieldy and inconvenient precursors of coins. Most have now been lost, though a few survived to be moved around between various museums in Malvern and Worcester. Currency bars and coins indicate trade – though it is not clear whether they indicate some kind of local business or a passing trader burying his cumbersome wealth for later use. Either way, such hoards suggest that they were the equivalent of today's bank deposit facilities – perhaps they even had some kind of guard to protect them.

Legend surrounds the religion of the ancient Britons, and A.E.E. Jones envisaged the settlers here under the control of Druids in time of peace.[§] He saw them worshipping in groves of oak, the strength and durability of which made it an appropriate emblem of deity, and to the trunks of which sacrificial

---

* Jabez Allies, *Antiquities and Folklore of Worcestershire*, 1856, p.159.
† E. Ekwall, *Concise Oxford Dictionary of English Place-Names*, 1990.
‡ Brian Smith, *A History of Malvern*, p.3.
§ A.E.E. Jones, *Anglo-Saxon Worcester*, 1958, p.16.

victims were bound. Mark Bowden[*] remarks upon the lack of archaeological evidence on the hills perhaps indicating that they were used for rituals which left little for modern archaeologists to work on. In any event, as with so many aspects of this period, nothing can be stated with certainty about the religion of these people. The Romans, of course, brought their own religion, worshipping numerous deities and eventually, after years of persecution, tolerating and finally espousing Christianity.

When the Roman Emperor Claudius sent his highly trained professional legions to Britain in A.D. 43 Roman culture was gradually, and often painfully, imposed upon the native population. It appears, however, to have made little lasting impact in this region which was much later to become part of Worcester-shire and Herefordshire. Nevertheless, in 1847 nearly 300 brass coins, covered in verdigris and dating from A.D. 286 to 311, when the Romans occupied Britain, were found in two decayed pots at Little Malvern. They aroused some interest at the time, the local postmaster noting that 'coins were continually passing in letters through the post office'.[†] This is an indication of how casually archaeological finds were then treated, allowing many of the coins to be dispersed and effectively lost for ever. No-one knows who hid them, though they raise the long-standing question of the strength of Roman influence in this area. Worcester was probably a fairly small Roman settlement and rough pottery remains have been found north of Malvern Link. Bronze-Age and Roman relics were found when The Chase School and Safeway (now Morrisons) supermarket were built, but much more research is needed before any definitive conclusions can be made about the local impact of the Romans.

Nor is it evident why the Iron-Age settlers left the Malvern Hills about the time of the Roman invasion. It appears, however, not to have been a direct consequence of the invasion, the tale of Caractacus defying the fearsome power of the Roman army on British Camp being a legend encouraged by 19th-century locals keen to give Malvern some claim to glory. Being of the generation that believed the story – told on a plaque at the foot of British Camp – Edward Elgar, looking towards the hills from his summer home at Birchwood Lodge in Storridge, named one of his most famous works *Caractacus* after the great British hero. One, perhaps overly simplistic, notion has never been aired but is at least worthy of some consideration. It is that the Romans prided themselves on their *pax romana* – the Roman peace in regions subjected to their rule, which tolerated no rebellious spirit. In such circumstances, with the threat of attack removed, there was no need for any tribe to inhabit so exposed and inconvenient a site as the Herefordshire Beacon.

Although so little is known about these early years, it is clear that the Malvern landscape was already being adapted for human use and convenience, and that a good deal of local activity was going on before and during the Roman occupation of Britain.

After the Romans left Britain in the early fifth century, the way was open for Angles and Saxons to invade, bringing their own culture and beliefs. Southern Britain became England, land of the Angles, as the French *Angleterre* still more obviously indicates. After they defeated the British in 577 at Dyrham, north of

---

* Mark Bowden, *op. cit.*, p.14.
† Jabez Allies, *British, Roman and Saxon Antiquities and Folklore of Worcestershire*, 1856, p.165.

Bath, the invaders quickly overran the Severn Valley. This central part of England became home to several Anglo-Saxon tribes and the Malvern area found itself on the western borders of the territory of the Hwiccii people. It was part of a great forest in Mercia, the kingdom which occupied the central lands between the other two kingdoms of Northumbria, to the north, and Wessex, which then occupied southern Britain. In the seventh and eighth centuries there were numerous kings of Mercia, of whom the most famous were Penda (626-55) and Offa (757-96), but there was competition for control from another institution – the young and determined Christian church, which also needs to be seen in context.

The Anglo-Saxons had brought their own religion, names of their gods still being preserved in our names for the days of the week. Various Christian missionaries sought to convert Anglo-Saxon leaders, and legend relates that a meeting to resolve differences of doctrine was held between Christian leaders at Augustine's Oak. Such a portentous meeting has, over the years, fed many imaginations and community rivalry. Some people believe the spot to have been in nearby Alfrick, though no real evidence supports this story, and at least three other locations in Worcestershire have laid claim to the distinction. Differences between Christian leaders were eventually resolved at the synod of Whitby in 664, and the Christian church in England became part of the great church organisation headed by the pope in Rome. By the end of the seventh century two dioceses centred on Worcester and Hereford were formed, and the earliest churches set up in emerging parishes. Ecclesiastical organisation was ahead of the shires or counties of civil administration, giving the church an important base from which it was later to exercise power not only over matters spiritual but also over material and political affairs. Much research is still needed on the period often referred to as the Dark Ages, though numerous charters relating to grants of land have already been translated and published by scholars such as Della Hooke, proving that parish and shire boundaries were established well before the Norman Conquest. The Malverns were an obvious physical boundary to separate the counties of Herefordshire and Worcestershire, an early medieval division that remains to this day, though during the closing years of the 20th century the two counties were administratively united. This unhappy union lasted less than 30 years, scarcely registering on the time scale of their long independent history.

When another invader came in 1066 extensive woodland still covered the plains below both the eastern and western slopes of the Malvern range. Not long after his victory at Hastings William the Conqueror designated the wilderness around Malvern as one of several royal hunting grounds. His decision, probably made in the early 1080s, about the same time as the foundation of Great Malvern Priory, had an impact which he could not possibly have foreseen. His Malvern Forest, with all the legal implications of that status, was to restrict development of an extensive area for the next 550 years.

Since medieval times William the Conqueror's forest has, rather confusingly, been more often referred to as Malvern Chase. In fact both Forest and Chase are acceptable terms but there is a significant distinction to be made between them. If a monarch reserved the hunting rights for himself, the area over which they were exercised was designated a forest. But if he granted his hunting rights to a subject – and William the Conqueror's successors often did – the area lost the status of a royal forest and became a chase, the grantee becoming lord of the chase.

7 Thomas Habington as depicted in Dr Nash's Worcestershire.

Malvern was actually a royal forest for less than 200 years, whilst it was a chase for nearly 400 years, so it is easy to see why Malvern Chase is the more frequently used name. It was not long after William the Conqueror's af-forestation that his grandson, Henry I (1100-35), made his own illegitimate son, Robert Fitzroy, lord of the chase of Malvern. The lordship remained with his descendants throughout the 12th century. There is a brief period at the beginning of the 13th century when ownership is difficult to establish, but the lordship – and hence forest rights – was not returned to the Crown until the end of the 15th century. The Crown retained them until Charles I decided to disafforest in the 17th century.

The precise descent of the ownership of the rights is complicated. Following it is a tedious and not very rewarding business, even with the benefit of research done by the 17th-century historian Thomas Habington,* his 18th-century successor Dr Treadway Russell Nash and the 20th-century compilers of the *Victoria County History*. Nevertheless, a history of Malvern Forest and Chase must try to unravel some of its intricacies and attempt some overview of events.

Robert Fitzroy's rights were inherited by his son and then his grand-daughter Elizabeth (another confusion being that she was sometimes referred to as Isabella, the continental version of the name). Elizabeth was married to John, who eventually became King John in 1199. John liked being in Worcestershire, and his

---

* Habington had been involved in the Gunpowder Plot of 1605 and was fortunate to escape a death sentence. His rather pleasant punishment was to be confined for the rest of his long life (1560-1647) to Worcestershire, where he amused himself (and earned the gratitude of later historians) by attempting to write the first county history. A more comprehensive and systematic work was produced in the late 18th century by Nash.

wish to be buried here when he died was carried out – his tomb is in Worcester Cathedral. He ordered a castle to be built at Potters' Hanley, thus causing that settlement to become known as Hanley Castle. When John's marriage with Elizabeth was dissolved (because of controversy over their being first cousins) the terms of the divorce ensured that John kept the partially built castle. The lordship of Hanley, with rights in the chase, went to his ex-wife and her new husband, Geoffrey de Mandeville.* When she died her sister Amice inherited the lordship of Hanley and passed it to her son by her husband, Richard de Clare. This son, the first 13th-century Gilbert de Clare and also Earl of Gloucester, was given the castle by King John's son, Henry III. Both the lordship of Hanley and the chase rights remained in the hands of successive de Clares throughout the 13th century. When the last Gilbert de Clare was killed in 1314 at Bannockburn his sister Eleanor inherited.

Eleanor de Clare's possessions then came into the hands of her husband, Hugh le Despenser, favourite of King Edward II, and their descendants. Through marriage into the Despenser family the Beauchamp family – earls and dukes of Warwick – inherited the Despenser possessions. Warwick the Kingmaker featured prominently in the power struggle between Yorkists and Lancastrians in the 1480s culminating in the bloodshed of the Wars of the Roses from which Henry VII, the first Tudor monarch, emerged triumphant in 1485. Determined to keep hold of the throne by every means, he sought through marriage to combine peacefully the interests of both sides, but was also driven to violent measures. Feeling threatened by the strong claim to the throne of the young Earl of Warwick, Henry had him imprisoned. In 1499 he had him executed for a conspiracy of which this unfortunate youth, who had spent most of his short life in prison, understood little. Henry retained forest rights in Malvern for the Crown, which kept them until the 1630s though, as we shall see, successive monarchs had virtually no idea of what was happening here.

---

* *Victoria County History,* Vol. IV, 1924, pp.93-4.

II

Origins and Boundaries
of Malvern Chase

Much of medieval Worcestershire was forest: during the Norman and Plantagenet periods it contained four named forests – Feckenham, Horewell, Ombersley and Malvern. In addition, four other forests – Corse, Wyre, Kinver and Arden – in neighbouring Gloucestershire, Shropshire, Staffordshire and Warwickshire included parts of Worcestershire.

The reasons for choosing particular areas for afforestation are not always clear, but in the case of Malvern Forest, the seat of administration of which was Hanley, the fact that William the Conqueror held the manor of Hanley may be significant. Domesday Book records that 'The King holds Hanlie. Brictric held it'. There is a story, probably much embellished and possibly totally fictitious, of the king's acquisition of Hanley.[*] In the reign of Edward the Confessor (1042-66) Hanley was in the hands of Brictric Snow, Lord of Tewkesbury and latest in the line of influential nobles of the midland region that had once been the great kingdom of Mercia. Brictric, highly regarded by the royal court before the Conquest, had been sent by King Edward as ambassador to the Count of Flanders. When in Flanders he rejected the amorous advances of Matilda, who later married William the Conqueror but never forgot Brictric's rejection. Seeking revenge shortly after the Conquest, she urged her husband to confiscate the manors held by Brictric, who died in prison shortly afterwards.

Just as the provenance of this story is not clear, so the boundaries of Malvern Forest are not clear, and probably never will be. Indeed, as Lord Eversley noted, 'with two exceptions [the New Forest and Hampton Court] the origin of royal forests in England is lost in antiquity'.[†] Medieval records give insufficient evidence for any definitive statement of the precise boundaries of William the Conqueror's Malvern Forest. Later monarchs so greatly increased areas throughout the realm subject to forest law that in the early 13th century there were about 143 forests in England.[‡] Since agriculture was expanding, pressure was put on the Crown by the Forest Charter of 1217 to reduce them to the boundaries of Henry II's reign, which had ended in 1189. Thus, by the end of the 13th century, in Worcestershire not only had Ombersley and Horewell forests been disafforested in 1229, but Feckenham forest had been reduced in size.[§] Probably the Conqueror's forest of

---

[*] W. Salt Brassington, *Historic Worcestershire*, 1894, p.127.
[†] Lord Eversley, *Commons, Forests and Footpaths*, 1910, p.157.
[‡] Oliver Rackham, *The Last Forest*, 1998, p.39.
[§] R.H. Hilton, ed., *Swanimote Rolls of Feckenham Forest*, 1960; and T.R. Nash, *Collections for a History of Worcestershire*, Vol.I, p. lxix.

Malvern, too, had been expanded and later reduced, making its boundaries even more difficult to define precisely. To this day one spot on the hills is called 'the Purlieu', pronounced locally as 'purley' – a term used to describe land illegally taken into a forest or disafforested land on the edge of a forest.

Surviving 16th-century documents indicate that by the 1580s at least 13 parishes had land in Malvern Forest or Chase. These parishes were Hanley Castle, Great Malvern, Little Malvern, Welland, Castlemorton, Birtsmorton, Berrow, Bromsberrow, Upton, Longdon, Leigh, Mathon and Colwall. Most were in Worcestershire on the eastern side of the Malvern range, but Colwall and Mathon were on the western side, while 103 acres of land in Bromsberrow were in Gloucestershire. A perambulation record of 1584[*] shows that other areas such as parts of Powick in Worcestershire were included, a reminder that in Saxon times the extensive parish of Powick included Great Malvern, Newland, Madresfield and part of Bransford.[†] An enquiry in 1558[‡] also included Baldenhall in the Chase: Baldenhall was the first Saxon settlement at Malvern, its importance declining in the later middle ages.[§] The area has again become more populous since with its modern name of Hall Green it is the site of the housing development on the Guarlford Road.

In medieval times monarchs granted hunting rights to the bishops of Hereford not only in Colwall, which was defined as part of Malvern Chase, but also in and around Ledbury and Eastnor, which were not. In 1630, preparatory to disafforestation, instructions to royal commissioners[¶] clearly stated that there were two distinct parts of Malvern Chase: the King's Chase in Worcestershire and Gloucestershire and the Bishop's Chase in Herefordshire. In addition, Corse Lawn abutted Malvern Chase so the total area of forest was very extensive.

It is unlikely that we shall ever be really clear as to the exact area which comprised Malvern Chase. Indeed, the 1630 officials were charged with the task of finding out the answer to that very question, so the precise boundaries were not known then and appear never to have been defined by any officials. The only certainty is that thousands of acres in three counties provided a vast tract for hunting, and were subject to forest law.

The definition of an area as a chase or a forest conferred a legal status rather than offering a description of the vegetation in a geographical area. It meant that the area was subject to forest law, which was framed specifically to protect the venison and the vert – the deer and anything in the forest which had a green leaf. The over-vert meant the great trees and the under-vert meant the bushes, gorse, thorn and fern.[**] The convenience of even the most powerful feudal tenant took second place to that fundamental principle of protecting the venison and the vert. Since the Domesday Book entry for Ripple and Upton-upon-Severn records that pre-Conquest bishops of Worcester hunted here, presumably there were either large red deer, the adult males of which were known as harts and the females as hinds, or the smaller roe deer in this area. Both were native to Britain but were eventually outnumbered by fallow deer – yellowish-brown with light

*   See Chapter 8.
†   Brian S. Smith, *A History of Malvern*, 1964, p.16 and Della Hooke, *Worcestershire Anglo-Saxon Charter Bounds*, 1990, p.214.
‡   WRO BA1751 705:295/2.
§   Brian S. Smith, *op.cit.*, pp.21-2.
¶   WRO 714 228.102/1.
** John Noake, *Worcestershire Relics*, 1877, p.178.

spots – introduced, probably by Henry I, in the early 12th century.[*] John Noake referred to the main beasts of the chase as including wild boar, hares, wolves and foxes. The much more scholarly Oliver Rackham[†] raises a more fundamental issue, questioning how fond medieval kings really were of hunting, which was a skilled sport. Certainly, however, ownership of forest rights empowered them to confer highly prized status symbols and consequent wealth upon favoured subjects.

Settlement had already taken place long before the Norman Conquest, so William the Conqueror's afforestation meant that established communities found themselves inconvenienced by forest laws which were imposed with varying degrees of harshness for the next 550 years. Even so important a personage as the Bishop of Worcester became obliged to recognise that the forest law limited what he might do with the manors he held here. It must have been particularly galling to him since, before the Conqueror set up his forest, bishops of Worcester had not only had the right to hunt here but also enjoyed the right to honey produced by the local bees. This was a valuable right in those pre-sugar days, and a useful source also of beeswax.

William ordered the Domesday Survey when he was at Gloucester for Christmas 1085, about two or three years after he seems to have decided on afforestation. One can well imagine him having an excursion from Gloucester that winter to see how things were going in his new forest in the area known as Malferna, and certainly the Domesday Survey shows that significant progress was being made. In Upton

> The woodland is half a league long and three furlongs wide and is in Malferna. [The bishop] had the honey from it and the hunting and all profits plus ten shillings; now it is part of the King's forest; but the Bishop has the pannage and wood for firing and repairs. It was and is worth £10.

The Domesday survey for Herefordshire shows that by 1086 two foresters, one from Bushley and one from Hanley, had been put by Earl William outside his manors 'to guard the woodland'.[‡] There were also tracts of land described as leagues of woodland in Hanley, Longdon, Powick and Upton in Worcestershire, in Cradley, Eastnor and Ledbury in Herefordshire and in Bromsberrow in Gloucestershire. Evidence of the appearance of some law enforcement is indicated by the noting of *riders*: one in each of Colwall, Cradley, Ledbury and Longdon, two in Mathon and no fewer than eight in Powick. Even allowing for some possible inaccuracy, it is clear that forest administration was getting underway. It is even possible that the Norman castle, with a wooden tower, added to the top of the Herefordshire Beacon was more of a hunting lodge than the military post that it has so often been assumed to be.[§]

It has been suggested that Hanley Forest would have been a more appropriate name than Malvern Forest. At the time of the Conqueror's afforestation Malvern was an insignificant settlement so remote from civilisation that the chronicler William of Malmesbury described it in the 12th century as a wilderness. In the 17th century Thomas Habington delightfully wrote:

---

[*]   Oliver Rackham, *The Last Forest*, 1998, p.47.
[†]   *ibid.*, p.51.
[‡]   John Morris (ed), *Domesday Book*, Vol. 17 for Herefordshire, 1983.
[§]   Mark Bowden, *The Malvern Hills, An Ancient Landscape*, 2005, pp.35-6.

> Maluern hyll … mountethe much in huge rockes leavinge in forepassed tymes belowe suche a wourld of trees overshawedeinge bushy thickets as William of Malmesbury wrytinge in the raygne of the Conqueror callethe it the Wyldrenes of Maluern.[*]

Clearly, it was ideally suited to the needs of the Benedictine monks who, seeking seclusion from the world, founded the priory at Great Malvern at about the same time as the forest was designated. Little Malvern Priory was founded about 40 years later. Malvern was not, however, the seat of forest administration. That distinction was enjoyed by neighbouring Hanley, the settlement known until the 13th century as Potters' Hanley, a place of considerable economic and social importance, because of its pottery industry deep in the heart of the forest.

Hanley appears twice in Domesday Book, one entry being in the Herefordshire folios and the other in the Gloucestershire folios. This was probably due to change of ownership of the manor, the two entries underlining the fallacy of the old belief that Domesday Book was utterly reliable, for there are differences in the two entries. It is not appropriate here to explore in depth the causes of the recorded differences, but it is worth remembering that the pressures under which the clerks worked increased the likelihood of error. William wanted the survey produced quickly, so speed probably led to clerical error, as did language problems. The clerks, whose native language was often French, wrote down their findings in abbreviated Latin, having received the information from local inhabitants who spoke in varying Anglo-Saxon dialects. Since the survey was completed in about eight months and travel was difficult – especially in winter and spring – it is astonishing that so much was achieved, for a fairly clear picture of many areas may be drawn. For example, there is enough information on Hanley common to both entries, to suggest a busy community of about 48 to 52 working people plus their families. There was a water-mill and woodland. The Herefordshire entry gives further proof that the forest organisation had already started, estimating that 'the woodland is 5 leagues reckoning length and width'. This is difficult to put into modern measurements, as a league might be anything from about one and half miles to three miles. The Domesday Book entry mentions the existence of an important facility for hunters and the presence of a forester holding about 15 acres: 'There is a hawk's eyrie. The forester holds half a virgate of land'. The Gloucestershire entry refers to a hay or haia, an enclosure probably used for fattening deer. It also states that its pre-Conquest value of £15 has fallen to £10, making it the same as that of the combined manors of Ripple with Upton, which had remained constant at £10. There is no explanation of the decline in Hanley's value, but perhaps the incorporation of most of the parish into the forest was deemed to have reduced its value. Those who had the right to hunt did not own all the afforested land, but the owners of land within a forest faced serious restrictions on what they might do with it and serious inconvenience from the effects of forest law.

Whilst some land had been laboriously cleared or settled before afforestation, no more land in the forest could be cleared for farming or housing without permission from the king or the lord of the chase. Permission to clear forest land was sometimes granted and, since a fee had to be paid for such a licence, it was a useful source of revenue for the lord of the chase. Nevertheless, forest law

---

[*]   Habington, *Survey of Worcestershire*, p.267.

effectively froze development in a very large area for the next twenty or thirty generations – which is a very long time. William the Conqueror himself probably permitted the clearing that became Newland, a significant name derived from the *nova terra* claimed from the forest. In the very heart of the chase, in the parish now known as Hanley Castle, some clearance probably took place in areas such as Gilbert's End in the 12th century. Certainly in 1189 Richard I, the Lionheart, freed 34 acres in Upper Welland from forest exactions, and in 1196 he also allowed the Bishop of Worcester to extend his forest clearings by a further 300 acres.* Such clearing was known as assarting, which explains the origin of Upper Welland's Assarts Road and Sarts Farm. In the absence of today's mechanised labour, any forest clearance was intensely hard work, requiring quite an army of men.

The forest was now established. How was it to be controlled?

---

* *Victoria County History,* Vol. IV, pp.442-3.

III

Forest Authorities

In the late 18th century Dr Treadway Russell Nash spent nine years producing what he modestly called Parochial Collections towards a History of Worcestershire. It was a time when antiquarian writing was held in low esteem[*] and he himself commented that a county historian is by profession a dealer in small ware. Initially seeing himself as a collector of information from others rather than an original researcher, he augmented the findings of the 17th-century historian, Habington, producing a much more comprehensive survey of the county. He wrote to Worcestershire incumbents, asking in a questionnaire for information on each parish. He found, however, that he needed to do a great deal of research himself and included chapters surveying the forests, rivers and other aspects of the county. It was all much more than he had anticipated:

> When I first undertook this work, it did not appear so troublesome or expensive as
> I afterwards found it; but having once begun, I determined to persevere.

He is now very highly regarded: his two great volumes, which now command high prices as antiquarian treasures, form an invaluable reference work for any serious Worcestershire historian.

They include his transcription of ancient documents, copied in a 16th-century handwriting from earlier writings.[†] He also summarised their key points, thus providing significant information and comment on the customs of the chase, and setting into context important 16th-century archives to be considered in later chapters of this book. He explained that the chase and the manor of Hanley belonged to the Crown, which had put them into the hands of the Earl of Gloucester:

> these customs and liberties, with many other, have been continued, and peace
> ably used since the time of Sir Gilbert de Clare, called the Red Earl, also earl of
> Gloucester, of whom as is aforesaid the said lordship is holden. For which liberties
> and customs, with many other, the aforesaid tenants and inhabitants consent and
> do pay yearly unto the lord thereof, LXVI. VIII.

There were special privileges for Hanley, whose

> Tenants and inhabitants are free to buy and sell throughout all England without
> payment of toll, custom, passage or pontage.

---

[*] D.C.Cox, *This Foolish Business, Dr Nash and the Worcestershire Collections*, 1993.
[†] WRO BA1751 705:295/2.

8   *Dr Treadway Russell Nash, as portrayed in his own* Collections for a History of Worcestershire.

The original documents, which stated that the lord appointed the constable of the castle at Hanley, cannot have referred to a period before the 13th century because the castle at Hanley was not built until King John ordered it in the early 13th century. The lord also appointed the officials who ensured that forest law was observed. These included the parker who supervised Blackmore Park, which was emparked (enclosed) for the fattening and preservation of deer in the early 14th century and probably much earlier. Malvern Forest contained several such parks. Brian Smith has noted them and others outside the apparent boundaries of the chase,[*] mentioning Blackmore, Cliffey, Colwall, Cowleigh, Farley, Hanley, Mathon, Parkwood and a small park in Powick, originally belonging to Worcester Cathedral Priory but given in 1314 to the prior of Great Malvern. John Noake[†] explained how parks were entered by deer leaps, citing Hindlip (hind leap) as an example on the edge of Feckenham Forest of how such features could explain place-names. Fences and ditches were an effective way of preventing deer from going in or out of parks. There were also hayes, enclosures into which game might be driven and slain. Every three weeks a court baron took place, as well as an annual law-day:

---

[*]   Brian S. Smith, *A History of Malvern*, 1964, pp.28, 32-3.
[†]   John Noake, *Worcestershire Relics*, 1877, p.193.

> The lord of the lordship of Hanley was chief lord of this chase, and of all the royalties of it, and maketh the constable of the castle of Hanley, the parker of Blackmore, the steward, the bailiff, the master of the game, four foresters and a ranger, to hold once in the year a law-day, and a court baron every three weeks, to determine all manner of pleas of trespasses, debts or detainer, which exceeded not the value of forty shillings.

Nash indicates that the Hanley court exercised power independent of other authorities:

> No sheriff, escheator or any other foreign officer whatsoever had any power to intermeddle within the said lordship; but the bailiff of Hanley was to execute and serve all precepts, and to return the same at his jeopardy ...

Anyone who illegally entered the lordship would be fined 6s 8d, which was one third of a pound.

Normally, serious crime was dealt with by Justices in Eyre, who travelled round to hear cases in county courts. In the forest, however, even in the event of serious crime, proceedings were taken by forest officials:

> The foresters only had authority to arrest every felon for felony and murder found within the said chase, and they were to bring him before the chief forester.

The chief forester, who was directly responsible to the lord of the chase and of Hanley, wielded great power and raked in large rewards. He had to pay his own costs and those of one other mounted forester and two footmen. He also, however, enjoyed a third of the proceeds of forest fines, large quantities of wood, the right shoulder of every deer killed in the chase, hens at Christmas and eggs at Easter. These comments by Nash are reinforced by the terms of sale of the forestership in 1480.[*] The sale also mentions other privileges such as the right to market beasts killed in the chase, interest in unmarked pigs, a portion of animals found straying in the chase and the power to appoint and supervise the foresters of the Hook and Cliffey areas. A considerable acreage of land and a house – presumably Hanley Hall in Gilbert's End – was another attraction. It was a most desirable post carrying all kinds of benefits which conferred social standing in a community where housing, food and clothing were, for most people, of very basic quality.

The office seems to have been hereditary in the Hanley family from the late 12th century until sold in 1480. Dissent and acrimony seem to have prevailed for the next generation or so, but after the office was bought in 1543 by Sir John Russell of Strensham his family retained it until the mid-17th century. An axe and a horn were the very appropriate symbols of the office, to be used in earnest as instruments of ultimate punishment and forest life, a little ceremony being recorded when the office was conveyed to trustees in 1480:

> At a place called the Swete Oke ... Richard Beauchamp, being in possession of the master forestership ... sitting at the said place, having the horn about his neck in sign and token of his true and peaceable possession in the said office and the axe in his hand for justice to be done with in the same office, the horn and axe were delivered to the three trustees and the horn blown out by Edmund Hewis, forester of the Hook.[†]

---

[*] James P. Toomey, *Records of Hanley Castle c.1147-1547*, 2001, Doc. no. 197.
[†] *ibid.*, Doc. no. 200.

Nash explains further:

> The chief forester … held of the chief lord in fee by a certain rent of an axe and an horn, and he had power to sit in judgement on the said felonies and murders, as also to execute the office of a coroner; and if the persons tried were found guilty by the verdict of 12 men, thereupon charged and sworn of the next four townships adjoining unto the place where the said felony and murder was done, his head was to be struck off with the forester's axe, at a place called the Sweet Oaks within the said chase, where they always sat in judgement on such persons and the body was to be carried unto the height of Malvern-hill, unto a place called Baldeyate, and there to be hanged on a gallows and so to remain unless licence were granted by the chief forester to take it down.

Some criminals were executed at the Rhydd, where the road from Malvern and Guarlford joins the main Upton to Worcester road. This might happen if a murder occurred within the part of Hanley over which the constable of the castle exercised authority.

One may assume that serious felonies and murders were out of the ordinary. The regular work of the forester was, for example, to fine anyone cutting down wood, at any time of the day or night, making sure that the fine was a fair one. If a non-commoner took wood the forester was to take the offender to the castle at Hanley, 'there to stand before the lord's grace and his officers'. A constant theme in forest law was to give every encouragement to officials to ensure that it was enforced. The forester was therefore rewarded if a successful prosecution was brought but had himself to pay the sizeable fine of £1 5s. if he were so remiss as to fail to take action against the offender.

A more serious offence arose

> If any of the foresters find any person or persons hunting within the said chase…or standing suspiciously…with hounds drawing, or bloody hands, the same forester shall attach him or them and bring them unto the castle of Hanley, there to remain prisoners in a place called Bandbury chamber until they have found sureties.

The seriousness of this situation is apparent when we note that the sureties must be of £5 in value – a sum so colossal in medieval terms that no peasant was likely to earn it in his whole life. John Noake[*] elaborates on the expressions in the above quotation from Nash: to be caught in the act of committing an offence could mean that the offender was *stable standing*, or standing with his bow ready to shoot. *Dog-draw* was when the beast had been struck and a dog was moving towards it, and *back bear* was when the dog was actually carrying it away. *With bloody hands* is self-explanatory and certainly not a happy position in which to be found.

There are horrifying tales that forest offences carried ferocious punishments such as blinding by gouging out of eyes, amputation of hands and castration. In practice this seems unlikely to have happened very much, if at all. Such barbarities were, in any case, forbidden by the Forest Charter of 1217, forced upon the nine-year-old Henry III soon after his accession, just as his father John had been forced to sign Magna Carta two years earlier.[†] We do not know what happened specifically in Malvern, except that no evidence of such punishments

---

[*] John Noake. *Worcestershire Relics*, 1877, p.175.
[†] H.W.C. Davis, *England under the Normans and Angevins*, 1921, p.398.

has been uncovered. Oliver Rackham[*] claims that not a single case has been brought forward as evidence and that courts were interested in pence, not limbs, adjusting fines so as not to dry up the supply.

Under the chief forester were subordinate foresters and keepers of the various walks into which the forest was divided, such as Baldenhall, where Hall Green now leads from the Guarlford Road to a housing estate preserving some of the ancient names. Bruerne and Southwood walks encompassed the more southerly lands such as Berrow and Longdon while the Link walk covered the more northerly. Like the boundaries of the chase itself, the boundaries of the walks are far from clear. In each walk, in addition to the keeper, there were verderers, viewers and riders who were rather like policemen patrolling their beats and reporting offences. Verderers took their name from *vert*, meaning the green habitat they were protecting. Some of these officials were empowered and required to perambulate and inspect the forest by virtue of their occupation of certain land.

> There were also certain verderers, viewers and riders, which by their tenure and holding of land, had power to ride and perambulate the ground, soil and townships, of every lord, from the aforesaid Charmeys Pool unto Powykbridge and Braunceford Bridge, to oversee the highways and water-courses, and to take care that the wood hedges adjoining to the chase be lawfully made for the preservation of the deer.

The problem of dogs' natural tendency to chase deer led to their hombling:

> Also for the hombling of the dogs, the said viewers and riders were to have the oversight and correction thereof, twice every seven year, and such manner of dogs as were found unlawful, that is to say, could not be drawn through a certain sterop of 18 inches and a barley-corn in length and breadth compass, the farther joints of the two middle claws were to be cut clean away, and the master and owner of the dogs were to be amerced 3s 1d ...

John Noake[†] wrote that forest inhabitants were allowed to keep a dog, ingeniously suggesting that the term *mastiff* was a corruption of '*maze thief*' or thief frightener. He also gave graphic detail of the mallet, chisel and wooden block with which the hombling operation was performed.

Pigs were fattened in the autumn by foraging for acorns and beech mast or nuts. The benefits of this important right of pannage could sometimes be extended to those living outside the lordship:

> If there is much mast in the said chase, then the bailiff of the manor ... shall call before him the best of the tenants and inhabitants of Hanley ... and they with the foresters to go together and view the mast ... If there be found more mast than sufficeth to keep the tenants and commoners' swine, the bailiff thereupon to proclaim a tack in the market towns next adjoining the chase ... of which tack the lord ... shall have all the profits except the scoring pence of every one that bringeth swine to the ... tack; which said pence belongeth to the bailiff.

Every autumn, between Michaelmas and Martinmas, the bailiff and tenants would drive the chase to check that only animals belonging to those with

---

[*] Oliver Rackham, *The History of the Countryside*, 1997, pp.136-7.
[†] John Noake, *op.cit.*, p.176.

common rights were grazing. Clearly identification marks consisted of snicking the animals' ears for Nash states that

> if there be any swine found whole-eared or any foreigner's swine they shall all be forfeited and the lord shall have two parts and the chief forester the third part.

This division between the lord and the chief forester of the spoils applied also to unclaimed strays impounded in the pinfold. They were kept for a month but might be claimed by a commoner who would get them back only if he paid for the trouble caused.

Place-name origins are full of traps for the unwary, but the medieval documents indicate that now familiar names are very old and some are fairly clearly traceable to individuals. Robert de Hanley was chief forester in 1165 and probably gave his name to Robertsend Street, which is mentioned in a late 13th-century charter (*viam de Roberteshende*).[*] *Gilbertesendestrete* and *Pikenhende* are mentioned in other late 13th-century charters.[†] In the 17th century Habington mentioned Gilbert de Hanley whose *habitation is at thys daye called Hanley Hall*. The Lechmeres, who arrived in the 11th century, were at *Sevarnesende* in 1339[‡] when Henry Lechmere gave his son Robert property by the public quay – perhaps the point of departure for Hanley pottery to be delivered to places along the Severn.

The boundaries of the chase were never a matter of easy resolution. Nash greatly enhances our understanding of forest law, but unfortunately makes defining the boundaries of the chase even more complicated since Hanley animals were allowed to wander for miles:

> Tenants and inhabitants of Hanley … may common with their cattle from … Maysmore Bridge in the county of Gloucester unto Powick's Bridge and Brandsford's Bridge in the county of Worcester.

Perhaps this remarkable extent of grazing for Hanley animals was due to the medieval manorial lords of Hanley being successive earls of Gloucester who also had hunting rights in Gloucestershire.

Whatever the reason, Hanley lords had special privileges, including payments from landowners in Colwall and Mathon, who claimed that the payments entitled them to grazing rights in the Chase – a claim justified by evidence from 1558 when Mary Tudor and her husband, Philip of Spain, were trying to establish the value of their rights in the Chase.[§] Much later, in 1794, when Hanley wanted to enclose its commons, it obtained legal opinion stating that *certain Oats and Fowl Rents* had nothing to do with grazing rights. This opinion – far from unbiased – was that the rents were related to when

> the Lord of the manor who resided at his seat at Blackmoor Park in the midst of the Chase, when the whole Chase was a fforest and nearly covered with wood, kept Hounds to destroy vermin with which the Chase was much infested, and that the Inhabitants of Colwall and Mathon made these payments as contributary towards the expence of keeping the Hounds but the tradition does not extend to the adjoining parishes on the Hanley side of Malvern Hills which it might be supposed were equally bound to contribute.[¶]

---

* J.P. Toomey, *op.cit*. Doc. no. 19.
† *ibid*. Doc. nos.14 and 18.
‡ *ibid*.
§ WRO BA1751 705:295/2.
¶ WRO BA1533 705:79.

Hanley was certainly special and was the seat of administration holding the regular courts. Important office-holders and ecclesiastical dignitaries could appear at the court, including the *free suitors* who acted as arbiters if a plaintiff thought that there had been some misjudgement by the officials. There was, therefore, the possibility of decisions being overturned by the free suitors 'according to law and reason' since, 'if need required, the said free suitors were to be of counsayle at the said law-day'.

> To this court, besides the homage and customary tenants thereof, were free suitors, the abbot of Westminster, the abbot of Pershore, the prior of Much Malverne, the prior of Little Malvern, the lord Clifford for the lordship of Stoke upon Severn, the lord of Madresfield, the lord of Bromesbarow and the lord of Byrtes Morton. The bishop of Worcester had lands within this forest; for in the 8th of Richard I, John de Constantis, then bishop, had liberty granted him to assart in his own wood in the forest of Malvern, near to the mill of Wenland, 300 acres of land.

As we have seen, the Bishop of Worcester's right to assart enabled him to clear forest land. Successive bishops of both Worcester and Hereford were fully conscious of their rights in the chase, and were not intimidated by the ambition and apparently superior powers of the Earl of Gloucester. Nash gives details of the ancient quarrels of the earl with both bishops who robustly defended their rights. In dispute with the Bishop of Hereford as to the boundaries of his chase, the earl encroached upon the Bishop of Worcester's lands to build his famous ditch, nick-named the Red Earl's Dyke. An interesting solution was reached and ratified in 1290:

> These lands of the bishopric were it seems encroached upon by the trench made by the earl of Gloucester, on the top of Malvern-hill before mentioned, which by the mediation of Robert Burnel bishop of Bath and Wells, and others was thus ended, that the earl and his countess should pay yearly to the bishop and his successors a brace of bucks and a brace of does out of his chase at Malvern, at his palace of Kemsey; and in the vacancy of the see, the same to be paid to the prior and convent of Worcester, demanding them by their attorney at the Castle of Hanley.

This chapter has sought to outline the theoretical basis of law and life in the medieval forest. Other sources now need to be considered to produce a more detailed portrait of the realities and practicalities of life in Malvern Chase.

IV

Life in the Medieval Forest

E dwin Lees in his 1877 survey of Malvern Chase quoted from a 14th-century
letter written by Reginald Brian, Bishop of Worcester from 1352, reminding
the Bishop of St David's that he had promised to send him six brace of
hunting dogs. Excited as a child at the prospect of their arrival, he wrote:

> Let them come then, O reverend father, without delay; let my woods re-echo with
> the music of their cry and the cheerful notes of the horn; and let the walls of my
> palace be decorated with the trophies of the chase.

Like so many evocative comments, when critically examined, this actually
poses some interesting questions. First, where exactly did Bishop Brian hunt?
John Noake[*] points out that bishops of Worcester had three parks in the county
– at Alvechurch, Blockley and Hartlebury, the latter containing the episcopal
palace. Like other bishops, he clearly loved the sport. Did he receive invita-
tions to hunt with the Bishop of Hereford on the other side of the Malverns?
Did he pursue this passion in one of Worcestershire's other forests, perhaps at
Feckenham or Wyre? Or had the bishops of Worcester reached agreement with
the Earl of Gloucester, as lord of the chase, enabling them to hunt in Malvern
Chase or Corse Lawn? There may be a clue in an observation of Habington[†] who
recorded that, over a hundred years later, in 1459, Bishop John Carpenter

> dyd ... appoynt hys servant to bee hys woodward in Wenlond, and within the
> chase of Malvern, and collector of hys rentes theare, with xl[s] and sometymes iii[li] a
> yeere fee, and a lyvery gowne sutable to hys Gentellmen.

Clearly, the bishops had a serious interest in proper woodland maintenance in
Wenlond, which was the medieval name for Welland. The woodland held there by
successive bishops was valuable enough to justify the expense of a woodward and
the episcopal land there brought in useful rents, as we see above. One wonders
whether those paying rents and trying to farm their land shared Bishop Brian's
enthusiastic and romantic view of the joys of stag-hunting, which was obviously
a rich man's sport and likely to damage crops.

The poor had to be content with the more prosaic rights which belonged to
those who struggled to get a living from the soil, and for whom forest law exacerbated the struggle. The mid-14th century, when Bishop Brian was anticipating

---

[*] John Noake, *Worcestershire Relics*, 1877, p.195.
[†] Habington, *A Survey of Worcestershire*, p.454.

such fun, was a particularly bleak time. Poor harvests for prolonged periods had weakened resistance to epidemics of which the 1349 Black Death was the most terrible example. The resultant labour shortages undermined the traditional feudal bargain between lord and tenant, whose labour was the rent paid to the lord in return for some land. The loss of between a third and a half of the population led to increased use of money as labourers hired themselves out where they could get the best deal and thus effected permanent economic changes.

Noting such changes, it is appropriate to be alert to several differences between medieval and modern conditions. All farming entails hard work with uncertain results. But medieval farming – like that in undeveloped countries today – was hard manual labour with results so uncertain that hunger and disease regularly distressed and depleted the population. Average life spans were about half those of modern societies, and the average length of a marriage was about ten to fifteen years until one partner died, women of course being at particular risk from childbirth. Evidence in the records of Hanley Castle and Welland suggests that at least some, and possibly all, of the chase parishes had large arable fields growing crops such as wheat and barley. Divided into strips or selions distributed among the manor inhabitants, they were known as 'open' or 'common' fields, referring to the communal nature of the farming. These terms in medieval farming are different from the modern usage of 'common land' to imply uncultivated areas used for a variety of purposes. The tell-tale ridge and furrow markings of medieval arable farming lasted for generations all over the English landscape, though much caution needs to be exercised when identifying medieval ridge and furrow – there is sometimes confusion with later farming practices such as hop-growing. Each medieval field was given over to the raising of a particular crop, fertility being maintained by crop rotation and, after harvesting, allowing stock to graze, thus manuring the ground. Such organic farming was the only available system, the absence of modern chemicals and equipment as well as variations in the weather making it an occupation fraught with uncertainties.

Medieval farmers had a hard enough task in struggling against the elements. Under forest law their struggles were infinitely harder because they could not legally allow hedges to grow to a height that would stop deer trampling and eating crops. As they laboured at the exhausting work of cutting back hedges without benefit of modern mechanised hedge cutters they must have cursed at having thus to facilitate the depredations of the deer. They were not even allowed to hunt the deer off, being required instead to summon forest officials, who were unlikely to hurry themselves, enabling the deer to devastate the crops and go off to wreak havoc elsewhere. Whilst the farmers could not effectively protect their livelihood, huntsmen could benefit from protecting deer in the enclosed parks which existed in the forest. Medieval life might be said to have strange priorities.

When farming scarcely reached subsistence level, since life in a forest area where deer were allowed to roam freely was especially hard, rights and privileges which ameliorated conditions were highly valued. Every manor or parish – and parish boundaries were largely set before the Norman Conquest – contained inferior land which was not enclosed for arable farming and which could be used by the local inhabitants for a variety of purposes. Today we often call such land common land, a widely misunderstood term. It is often wrongly interpreted as land not only in public ownership but also carrying a vague expectation that anyone has the right to walk over it, pitch a tent, exercise a dog or, these days, park a car and pursue countless other activities on it. No medieval person would have imagined such freedom existing. As we have seen above, common fields were historically arable fields farmed in common by the residents of a parish. The land which we so loosely describe as common was more properly referred to as the waste or wasteland, and its use reserved for the inhabitants of the particular parish of which it was part. Since the use of wasteland was restricted, it was not for the benefit of anyone or any animal who happened to come along, so it was in a sense private. Somewhat unusually, within the area of Malvern Chase inter-commoning was practised, enabling all the constituent parishes to share their wastelands.

Grazing rights on wasteland have sometimes been overestimated by people ignoring the fact that often a stint was imposed, limiting the number of beasts put out to graze by any individual. Nevertheless, although numbers of stock were not as high as we may imagine, the monotonous and uncertain diet of medieval families was undoubtedly enhanced by the addition of fresh milk, butter or cheese, made possible by the keeping of an animal or two on the waste. Shortage of winter fodder necessitated an annual autumn slaughter of animals, ensuring, however, that sufficient were left for future breeding. The autumn cull provided a welcome, though probably modest, amount of meat which could be salted for use during the winter.

Special rules governed pigs, which can be quite savage and were forbidden in the forest for about a month in midsummer when does were giving birth and the young fawns were vulnerable. Some landowners were permitted to put their pigs in the woodland in the autumn when, in a good year, they put on weight by devouring some of their favourite foods – acorns and beech nuts. In 1086 Hanley had six swine herds paying a total of 60 pigs in rent for this valuable right of pannage. The usual rent was one-tenth of the total worth, so this suggests not only 600 pigs – a large number – but also many oak and beech trees. Since pigs did not necessarily enjoy a diet rich in acorns and beech nuts, those in this area appear to have been particularly fortunate. By 1548-9 some parts of the chase were said to be 'rotted up with swine' according to the notes made by the compilers of the *Victoria County History*.[*]

Venison from the forest was legally reserved for the lord of the chase but even such important men were likely to enjoy it at special feasts rather than as everyday fare. Naturally some reached dinner tables by dubious means: John Noake[†] points out that it was most discourteous to ask where venison came from if one was fortunate enough to be served it, quoting an old source with a side swipe at the clergy:

> It is no manners for him that hath good venison before him to ask whence it came, but rather fairly to fall to it; so hearing an excellent sermon, he never enquires whence the preacher had it, or whether it was not before in print.

Presumably there were spots in the forest where the old practice of charcoal burning provided a living, but it is scarcely mentioned in local literature and

---

[*] WRO BA527 899:44/26.
[†] John Noake, *Worcestershire Relics*, 1877, p.179.

seems therefore to have been less important than it was, for example, in the Forest of Dean. The main uses for charcoal in Malvern Chase were probably by potters heating their kilns and blacksmiths needing fuel for forges. The right to pick up windfall wood, which yielded material for both fuel and house repair, was valuable to all householders.

The dense woodland was not always a haven of peace and tranquillity, nor a safe place in which to find oneself. Malvern Forest was home to deer and many small woodland creatures but land adjacent to tracks occasionally sheltered thieves as well as large animals like cattle or wild boar. Although shy and retiring, if disturbed wild boar readily attacked men and women, and had been known to kill and eat young children. They had largely died out by the middle of the 13th century, Oliver Rackham believing that the last truly wild boar were in the Forest of Dean from where Henry III ordered the killing of 12 in 1260.[*] Wolves, too, preyed on anything that moved in the forest. Della Hooke[†] found reference to a wolf-fence in Longdon in the 10th century, and in the middle of the 12th century, during the reign of Henry II, payments were made to an official wolf-hunter.[‡] Much later, in 1327 a patent roll of the first year of the reign of Edward III shows that an individual called John de Sapy obtained a licence to hunt wolves and foxes in winter. He could do so in the Chases of Malvern and Corse, without impediment from the chase officials such as the foresters and verderers. This patent roll is thus also a useful reminder of the vast extent of the chase which stretched from Corse Lawn through both the Bishop of Hereford's chase and that of the Earl of Gloucester.

There was a perambulation of the Bishop of Hereford's chase in 1394 when Bishop Trefnant wanted to establish his rights. His chase included deer, partridge, pheasant and hare, while his Palace at Ledbury also had fishponds in the grounds to provide good food even on days of abstinence. Malvern Chase similarly would have been home for partridge, pheasant, probably introduced in the 11th or 12th century,[§] and pigeon, providing luxury foods for the rich, but constituting a plague to the poor, whose crops they devoured. Smaller animals included the rabbit, probably, according to Oliver Rackham, introduced into England at the same time as the fallow deer in the early 12th century, soon after William the Conqueror's afforestation but not in his lifetime. Used for both food and clothing, rabbits were encouraged by the provision for them of warrens, and were for the benefit of the rich landowner, not the poor. Although the rabbit was to become a pest to farmers and gardeners, it was highly prized in medieval times, when it was vulnerable and needed protection, not even being able to dig its own burrow.[¶] The existence of a rabbit warren, sometimes deliberately built in medieval times to protect and encourage the creatures, can be detected from place names such as Conygree, coney being an old name for a rabbit. Ledbury, of course, has its Coneygree Wood from which medieval bishops of Hereford enjoyed the benefits afforded by the rabbit. Rabbit later became more popular with the lower ranks of society. Until well into the 20th century a poor family could enjoy a tasty nutritious meal of stewed rabbit and use its fur for

---

[*] Oliver Rackham, *The History of the Countryside*, 1997, p.36.
[†] Della Hooke, *Worcestershire Anglo-Saxon Charter-Bounds*, 1990, p.199.
[‡] *Victoria County History* Vol. IV, p.442.
[§] Oliver Rackham, *op.cit.*, p.50.
[¶] Oliver Rackham, *op.cit.*, p.47.

some item of clothing – and all for a few pence (or even for nothing if willing to risk committing the crime of poaching). Today the rabbit is less popular and its burrowing is causing damage to ancient protected sites such as Midsummer Hill and British Camp.

Forest law was in operation from the late 11th to the 17th centuries. Although change occurred much more slowly than has been the case in the last century, the conditions prevailing in the 17th century were naturally somewhat different from those of the 11th as forest life adapted to the vicissitudes of nature and the evolution of manorial, clerical and royal power. Although no portrait of medieval life is static, the late 14th-century poet, William Langland, who had lived through the horrors of the Black Death and wrote his *The Vision of William concerning Piers the Plowman* in the vernacular, gives some clues as to the realities of life in this area. Langland spent much of his life in London, but there are strong grounds for believing that he was born locally and educated at Malvern Priory and that he put this local knowledge into his portrayal of rural life.

> In a somer season, when soft was the sun …
> And on a May morning, on Malvern Hills,
> Strange fancies befell me, and fairy-like dreams.

Given this prologue, it is all too easy to see the poem as romanticising the past but it actually shows a firm grasp of harsh reality as well as showing the countryman's appreciation of nature. Langland's 'fair field full of folk … of all manner of men, the mean and the rich' included 'poor people that suffer much through dearth and drought, woe in the winter time, for they lack clothes'. When gifts of fruit and vegetables were offered to Piers, 'hunger soon gobbled it all up and asked for more'. The medieval miseries of winter included cold sleepless nights punctuated by the need to get up and rock the cradle 'cramped in the corner'. People rose before dawn to start on the day's work, cleaning and mending, carding and combing wool, winding yarn or peeling rushes to make the little rush lights which scarcely pierced the gloom of their stuffy little shuttered huts. Work outside in the fields was very hard, but the beauties and mysteries of nature also provided some consolation. Beautiful flowers brought a variety of colours and scents, while animals and birds brought inexplicable mysteries such as who taught birds to build nests in which to lay their eggs and breed their young.

9 *Some boy sweeps are said to have sheltered in the Devil's Oak and, running out from it on a foggy morning, looked like young devils. Its name may derive from this (possibly totally fictitious) anecdote or from its strange shape. Picture by Edwin Lees (1877).*

10   *The Friar's Elm, which Lees believed to have been planted in the 16th century, stood until the mid-20th century on the Guarlford Road, close to the junction with Hall Green.*

11   *Lees also criticised excessive pollarding of elm trees, illustrating his point with what he called a battered pollard elm looking very sad in a field near the River Teme at Powick.*

Further evidence of what nature had to offer is afforded by Edwin Lees, whose numerous publications on the local landscape in the 19th century give useful indication as to what was likely to have been in the medieval forest. He found a wide variety of both evergreen and deciduous trees, making particular mention of yew, holly, ash, birch, elm, lime, maple, oak, poplar and, along ancient water-courses and brooks, willow and alder. The service tree, or sorb, of the mountain ash family, was also plentiful, as were lime trees in Bromsberrow, but beech and hornbeam were not 'native to Malvern Chace or any part of Worcestershire'. He made a particular point of the prevalence of alder bushes bordering

> every stream that flows from the hills … and the coppices at the bases of the hills, until the recent spread of villas and houses around Great Malvern, were crowded with alders. This tree, being too often lopped like the willow, becomes mostly dwarf and distorted, so that alders of any altitude or spread of bough are of rare occurrence, though as it is an enduring tree and will bear any hacking, and decays but slowly, the old stumps that remain by brook sides … must be of great age and belong to forest times.[*]

Lees commented on the mosses to be found in the area and on the importance of decaying trees to promote the growth of fungi. He was also interested in the under-wood and bushes, noting species like buckthorn, bramble, dogwood, guelder rose, hazel, juniper, sloe and spindle-tree, all too often cut down and thus unable to grow to any great size. He suggested that the

---

[*]   Edwin Lees, *The Forest and Chace of Malvern*, 1877.

ivy that invests the Ivy-scar rock on the North Hill must, from the name given it, have been there for centuries.

Lees also noted how frequently elders were planted, recording the medicinal uses to which their leaves, blossoms, berries, wood and bark have been put. Even into the 19th century elder was also believed to protect both humans and cattle from witches. Crab apples and wild pears were scattered through the woodland but these fruits were also cultivated in Worcestershire orchards from medieval times, establishing an early reputation for fruit growing referred to by Camden in his *Britannia*. Richard Gough particularly noted that

> The quantity of cherries brought to Worcester in a plentiful year is amazing: two or three tons are often sold on a Saturday morning before 5 o'clock in the morning.

Probably the Romans introduced cherry trees into Britain, and Lees found the common wild cherry scattered throughout the chase. Nineteenth-century coach travellers paid tribute to the high quality of the orchards by the side of the road between Powick and Newland.[*] Lees referred to a 'Barland Pear Orchard' which he believed must have been planted in the 17th century, about the time that Malvern Chase was disafforested. It seems likely that such planting increased once disafforestation removed restrictions on land use.

It seems reasonable to suppose that such native woodland flowers as now grow in the area were to be found in the medieval forest. These include bluebells, cowslips, primroses and wild orchids, adding their colour and scent in the manner suggested by Langland.

There were also more exciting features to be observed. Probably the first beacons were lit on the hills in medieval – or even prehistoric – times. During the 16th century beacons came into use nationally as signals that invasion was likely and people should prepare to resist attack. Macaulay, the 19th-century historian, wrote romantically that in 1588 'twelve fair counties saw the blaze on Malvern's lonely height', when the Spanish Armada threatened the nation. The Armada failed in its task, but England remained anxious about the intentions of foreign rulers. The 1628 map of the Malverns (see Chapter X) clearly marks, with little

---

[*] *The Leisure Hour*, 1856, p. 698.

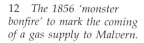
12   *The 1856 'monster bonfire' to mark the coming of a gas supply to Malvern.*

13 *The 1863 bonfire – probably to mark the marriage of Edward, Prince of Wales, to the beautiful Alexandra of Denmark.*

14 *Queen Victoria's golden and diamond jubilees were celebrated with bonfires.* The Malvern Advertiser *claimed that the Diamond Jubilee bonfire (1897) was 'the largest that has ever irradiated from Malvern's heights', enormous care having been taken to build it with 400 railway sleepers, 20 scaffold poles, 30 tar barrels, 2000 faggots and other materials, including liquid and consolidated petroleum.*

drawings and captions, beacons on the highest Malvern hill in Herefordshire and the highest in Worcestershire. Sufficiently noteworthy to be portrayed as landmarks in 1628, they were also marked on 18th-century maps. The name 'beacon' came to be incorporated into references to these two hills, while later bonfires on prominent hills became symbols of national celebration on occasions such as royal weddings or jubilees. This has happened on the Worcestershire Beacon into the 21st century.

V

Settlements in the Medieval Forest

lthough much of Malvern Chase – and much, indeed, of Worcestershire – was densely wooded, there were numerous settlements, some of them commercially thriving. Their commercial success continued and in some cases even increased after afforestation. Upton upon Severn, for example, appears in Domesday Book merely as part of the Bishop of Worcester's manor of Ripple. The joint manor had two priests, possibly one for each part of the manor, separated by the River Severn. This also suggests the existence of a church. The manor was worth a total of £10, the same value as that of Hanley which had declined from a pre-Conquest value of £15. This means that in the late 11th century Upton did not yet enjoy the commercial pre-eminence which largely resulted from its position on the River Severn. During a period of economic growth in the 12th and 13th centuries many new towns were founded by manorial lords keen to profit from rents and market tolls.[*] It seems very likely that successive bishops of Worcester created and developed such a town at Upton.

A prosperous medieval town like Upton, with episcopal support, could boast quite a grand stone church. Its

15 *The base of Upton's 'Pepperpot' tower is medieval, a lead-covered cupola having been added in the late 18th century. In 1814 the lead was replaced with copper. It is now a heritage centre.*

'Pepperpot' landmark is a survival of the, probably 14th-century, church tower, once topped by an elegant spire rather than the present copper-covered cupola.

---

* Christopher Dyer, *Bromsgrove: A small town in Worcestershire in the Middle Ages*, 2000.

31

Ecclesiastical landowners were superb estate managers and the bishops of Worcester were demonstrably keen to optimise their profits. In the neighbouring diocese successive bishops of Hereford from the mid-12th century transformed their manor of Ledbury into a flourishing town. Future historians need to examine evidence for similar intervention by the bishops of Worcester to develop Upton, which bears striking similarities to Ledbury, not least in its medieval burgage-style plots. Such long, narrow plots indicate maximisation of opportunities for trading outlets on the main street. Sometimes the rear of such a plot would be sub-let to another craftsman who had access from a back lane or via the passage at the side of the front shop. Tenancies would have appealed to craftsmen who would probably have been excused payment of market tolls and well prepared to pay the rents that filled the coffers of the efficient ecclesiastical land managers. Both Upton and Ledbury contain a New Street dating from medieval times, indicating a desire by the episcopal lords to cash in on the demand for commercial premises by extending the area laid out for craft and trade activities. Upton, again like Ledbury, had two distinct areas with different kinds of tenancies, some involved in trade in the town itself – the borough – and some in the more rural areas, often called the foreign. Ledbury and Upton served the needs of numerous surrounding settlements covering a radius of a few miles, and each maintained commercial pre-eminence over neighbouring villages for hundreds of years – a success not achieved by all towns founded by manorial lords. The Severn, a major thoroughfare comparable with a main motorway in modern times, gave Upton a particular advantage not enjoyed by Ledbury and other towns. Flowing down to the flourishing port of Bristol, it offered access to international trade: indeed, Bishop Swinfield of Hereford, with palaces at Ledbury and Bosbury, sent his men in the 13th century to collect his wine from Upton where it arrived by river from France. Such contacts with far-flung places would have been an exciting source of all kinds of tales for local people. Upton would also have attracted trade in agricultural produce such as grain and butter as well as in all kinds of skills and crafts, some associated with boat building as well as with arable and stock farming.

In early days the light portable coracle was much used on the Severn. Later the characteristic load-carrying barge was the trow, used until the late 19th century. This versatile vessel could sail with the wind, make use of the tide on the stretch from Bristol to Gloucester or be hauled by men or horses.

16 *This picture, from Salt Brassington's* Historic Worcestershire, *shows a 19th-century ferryman with his coracle.*

17 & 18   The modern pictures show the ease with which a coracle can be carried and an obviously enjoyable experience on a Castlemorton Common pond – rather different from working on the River Severn.

The Severn was also crucial in the commercial success of Upton's immediate neighbour, Hanley, pottery from which found its way by river to settlements along the Severn.[*] Hanley, a very large parish stretching from the Severn up to the top of the Malvern Hills, probably took its name from the Old English *hean leage* meaning 'at the high clearing'.[†] Its pottery trade caused it to become generally known as Potters' Hanley until the building of its castle at the beginning of the 13th century led to its new name of Hanley Castle. It is possible, though not proven, that Hanley, like Upton, had burgage plots in its central area, the hub of activity near the church. A Saxon church probably existed before the Norman Conquest and an unusual gravestone – the Lechmere stone – probably of Saxon origin, survives in the keeping of the Lechmere family.

[*]   Alan Vince, *Medieval and Post-medieval Ceramic Industry of the Malvern Region, Pottery and Early Commerce: Characterisation and Trade*, 1977, pp.275-92.
[†]   A. Mawer and F.M. Stenton, *The Place-Names of Worcestershire*, 1969.

19   This 18th-century print of Upton from Nash's Worcestershire *shows a trow on the River Severn.*

20 *Church End, Hanley Castle, as sketched in about 1822 by Maria Martin.*

21 *Hanley Castle church contains a mixture of building materials. This 19th-century drawing shows the less frequently seen view from the south east, the main entrance now being on the north side. Extensive 17th-century work used red brick, which is warm and welcoming as well as a reminder of the tile and brick making industry which brought commercial success to this region.*

Hanley had a market from at least the reign of Henry III, who changed the day of it from Tuesday to Thursday. The holding of a market was an important status symbol, requiring a royal charter. The market would be presided over by the local steward, so perhaps the steward of the castle was in charge of Hanley's market. The steward also usually presided over the Pie Powder Court, so called from the faltering attempts by Englishmen to pronounce the French *pieds poudreux.* The French expression means 'dusty footed' and is an indication of how plaintiffs and defendants may have looked at such courts, which gave immediate help to people who thought they had been swindled in the market. If travelling tradesmen cheated customers it was well-nigh impossible to bring them to justice in ordinary courts so the so-called pie powder courts were set up, usually meeting in the toll booth, or tolsey. Until at least the early 19th century the junction of Gilbert's End Lane, Robert's End Street and the main Worcester-Upton road was known by names suggestive of its having been the site of Hanley's toll booth. Old parish books and the 1797 Enclosure map refer to the spot variously as the Booth Hall Elm, Buthall Elm and Buthall Green, while Isaac Taylor's 1772 map shows the area as Boothend.

Hanley was clearly a hive of activity, made even more exciting by the building of the castle which figures so largely in the medieval documents of Hanley. Details of its history and appearance have been quite widely available since the publication of the fourth volume of *The Victoria County History* in 1924.* Built on the orders of King John, it seems to have had limited purpose as a strategically placed fortress, but was ideally situated as a spectacular hunting lodge. Such an unusual building would have given work to local masons, carpenters, metal workers and other specialist tradesmen. Indeed, maybe craftsmen came from far afield to seek work on such a project for the king himself.

Habington said that an assize court was held there as early as 1211-12, while Nash said in the 18th century that the court room had been on the site of what has now become the High School. The castle was damaged in 1321-2 when the Despensers were involved in the fighting between baronial factions under the weak Edward II, and an indenture of 1326 says that the abbots and monks of Evesham

> for benefits done to them by Sir Hugh Despenser ... undertake to find for him, his heirs and assigns a secular chaplain fit to sing mass and celebrate divine service daily in his castle of Hanley.

Some people have seen in this provision of a chaplain – and of books, vestments and *other things* – the origin of the school which has existed in the parish since medieval times, though the school is more likely to be of mid-15th-century origin.

Another puzzle is that the *Victoria County History* suggests that extensions were made to the castle around 1349, which seems surprising as the Black Death was then ravaging the country and labour was in short supply. The 1416 dower agreement for Eleanor, widow of Richard le Despencer, gave her a third of what seems to have been a large, pleasant and well equipped castle. She was granted

---

* *Victoria County History*, Vol. IV, pp.93-4.

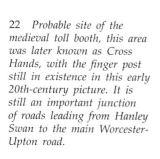

22 *Probable site of the medieval toll booth, this area was later known as Cross Hands, with the finger post still in existence in this early 20th-century picture. It is still an important junction of roads leading from Hanley Swan to the main Worcester-Upton road.*

> A great room at the end of the hall to the west with two towers of stone annex'd the said hall with one third of the pantry and buttery under the said room ... two rooms called les guesten chambres, three towers in the south with a fourth tower in the corner of the castle towards the south, a third part of the bakehouse and kitchen adjacent to the said tower ... with a third of the palisade and moat adjacent to the said four towers towards the south ... [and] ... free entrance and exit to the chapel.

In 1480-1 the gate-house, drawbridge, pool, mill and floodgate were repaired at a cost of £4 17s 10d, and in 1481-2 the chapel and kitchen were repaired. After Henry VII took over the castle it was allowed to fall into disrepair. Leland, the chronicler who died in 1552, suggested that it was deliberately vandalised by Sir William Compton, appointed by Henry VIII as castle constable:

> Syr John Savage and his father and graunt-father lay much aboute Hanley and Theokesbyri as keepers of Hanley. The erles of Gloucester were owners of this castelle, and lay much there. Mr Cometon clene defacid it yn his tyme beying keeper of it after Savage.[*]

By the 17th century Habington sadly noted:

> This Castell where the Earls of Gloucester lived and the Duke of Warwick dyed is so vanished as there appearethe nothing in that place but a littell rubbyshe and a seelly barne to teach us that the glory of this world vanishethe to nothinge. [†]

Clearly uninhabitable by Habington's time, the castle belonged to the Badger family who lived at Pool House on the main road from Worcester into Upton. Habington observed that 'the ruinated Castle and Parcke of Hanley have come to the Badgers, whom I wyshe happely to keepe them.' Nothing is now visible of the castle, its last remaining tower having been used in 1795 by its then owner, Thomas Hornyold, to repair a bridge over the Poolbrook, a tributary into the River Severn near Upton. In the 17th century

> a substantial house was built on the north side of the castle plateau ... and by degrees the turfy mounds have been cleared away, and a pretty, fertile garden occupies the site where once rose the massive towers.[‡]

That house and garden have now gone and, disappointingly, the site has never been systematically excavated, though Emily Lawson claimed in 1884 that

> some years ago a considerable extent of the foundation walls, nine feet thick, was laid bare, but ... covered up again without ... making a plan.

She also wrote of objects found in the moat – old wine bottles, a spur and a small dagger, but her most interesting reference is to a 'curious old windmill, the base of which was an enormous oak on which the mill worked with rollers'. Modern work with metal detectors has revealed nothing of significance.

One of the oldest schools in the country was founded in Hanley Castle, probably in the mid-15th century though, as observed above, a poorly authenticated

---

* Quoted by John Chambers in his *History of Malvern*, 1817, p.226.
† WRO BA527 899:44/26 (Notes made by the compilers of *The Victoria County History*).
‡ Emily Lawson, *The Nation in the Parish*, 1884, p.209.

claim has been made that it was as early as 1326. The foundation of schools in the medieval period is often a sign of prosperity, and Hanley's school adds another feature to the picture of a thriving settlement – almost an early town – in the forest. Although details of the school's foundation are not clear, it may be significant that prayers for the potters of Hanley were included in commemoration services up to modern times, suggesting a tradition that well-to-do potters sought to procure an education for their sons by establishing a grammar school. Nineteenth-century attempts to ascertain the purpose of the foundation – a grammar school for the sons of affluent tradesmen or an elementary school to teach all village children to read and write – reached no definitive answer. The former, however, seems much more likely, especially since the vicar was also the schoolmaster and was required to be *learned*.[*]

Inquisitiones post mortem[†], which were enquiries into the estates of recently deceased property owners, give more detail about Hanley and the forest inhabitants. The inquisition made after the death of Gilbert de Clare, Earl of Gloucester, in 1295 shows that 13 potters paid 6s 6d for clay at Michaelmas. When his widow and joint holder of the manor, Joan, died in 1307 there were only four potters paying two shillings, and when their son died in 1314 an unspecified number – probably 10 – were paying five shillings. The payment also mentioned dead wood, possibly for firing the kilns.

Although the lords of the manor of Hanley received various perquisites relating to the chase, most of the value lay in rents and services paid by tenants, of whom there were over 80, a number reasonably consistent with the 72 taxpayers named in 1280 taxation rolls. If multiplied by four – a common way of estimating the total population from limited numbers given in taxation rolls – a figure of about 300 people living in Hanley at the end of the 13th century is reached. Given the role of Hanley in forest administration and the value of its pottery industry, this number is likely to be much higher than most other chase parishes. All were to be significantly reduced by the famine and disease which wrought havoc and distress in the 14th century. National population figures were also affected by the 1290 expulsion of all Jews from England by Edward I. In Hanley in 1280 Richard Isaac and Reginald Abraham paid tax, but no such Jewish sounding names appeared in the tax roll of 1327, and one might ask if they had left or the families had simply died out.

The inquisitions afford insight into life in this large and important woodland settlement. In 1295, as lord of Hanley manor, the Earl of Gloucester enjoyed a *capital court with buildings, barton, garden and curtilage* worth three shillings. He had 151 acres of arable land, 28 acres of meadow for mowing and 17 acres of pasture land, the total value being over £4. In addition he had a pasture at Blackmore Park worth £1, as well as herbage and pannage worth £1 in the forest. The park itself will have been fenced in by a pale to keep the deer in. A windmill – quite a modern invention – was worth 13s 4d a year, the miller grinding the corn of everyone in the manor. Millers, holding a monopoly and suspected of keeping back flour for their own use, were notoriously unpopular and frequently the butt of jokes. One was

---

[*]   Pamela Hurle, *Hanley Castle, Heart of Malvern Chase*, 1978, Chapter 5.

[†]   J.W. Willis Bund, *Inquisitiones Post Mortem for the County of Worcester 1242-1326*, 1894 and James P. Toomey, *Records of Hanley Castle, c.1147-1547*, 2001.

What is the boldest thing in the world?
A miller's shirt for it clasps a rogue by the throat every day.

Rents and services from 32 customary tenants who each held six acres in vil-
leinage were worth nearly £11 a year, and the same amount was due from 51
customary tenants who presumably each held less. Adding in the £1 yearly value
of the pleas and perquisites of the forest the manor income was a most satisfactory £38 13s. 2¾d.

Nearly 20 years later, the 1314 inquisition gives a slightly higher total value
– £42 17s. 10¾d. – but £5 went on *repair of the houses of the castle* and the vicar
of Hanley *by ancient custom* received £1, a payment which underlines the importance of the church. Rents and other income in 1314 are comparable with,
but not identical to, those of 1295, though the value of arable land had dropped
from 4d. to 3d. per acre. Although there are some gaps in the document, the
tenants' services are indicated. Main services in the fields were winter ploughing
and harrowing, springtime sowing and, in summer and autumn, mowing and
reaping. But making hurdles, 'autumn carryings' and threshing were also vital.
At harvest time each tenant had to 'do 31 autumn carryings with carts, and the
value of the service is 2s 7d, value of each carrying 1d.' At Christmas 'they will
thresh...performing 104 works worth 11d, value of each work ¼d.' Malt making
and brewing were also required of the tenants.

A succession of cold stormy summers between 1308 and 1322 caused scarcity,
and in 1315 and 1316 there were famines.[*] The effects of this early 14th-century
distress and of the 1349 Black Death are suggested in the inquisition taken upon
the death of Hugh le Despenser in 1349. The value of the manor had gone down
by about 20 per cent, and 'the potters who used to render ... at Michaelmas
for having clay are dead, so they now render nothing'. The pottery trade was
revived – indeed the depredations made in the chase by potters in the 16th
century were to be criticised by John Hornyold[†] – but times were bleak and
frightening during and after the famines and plague.

Upton and Hanley were the most commercial parishes in the chase, but they
clearly also had extensive agricultural activity where conditions would have been
similar to those prevailing in other less developed parishes. Although, as we have
already noted, there can be confusion with later farming practices, archaeological
evidence – and particularly aerial photography – reveals the ridge and furrow
of medieval farming. At Birtsmorton, for example, archaeologists have pointed
to authentic medieval ridges, noting that place names such as street and green
suggest that the area was settled in the late Middle Ages.[‡] The standard bargain
of land in exchange for work would have been made with tenants in all manors,
while the wealth and influence of the church is evident from the number of chase
manors which had ecclesiastical lords. The influence of the clergy and the Roman
Catholic church is further evidenced by the number of churches to be found in the
chase from early in the period. Hunting rights and forest law were thus exercised
by kings and nobles over land which belonged to others, but even the most
powerful manorial lords had to pay due attention to the quite serious limitations
imposed by forest law. This made for a very interesting balance of power.

[*]   R.C.Gaut, *Worcestershire Agriculture*, 1939, p.45.
[†]   See chapter 6.
[‡]   Mark Bowden, *The Malvern Hills, An ancient landscape*, 2005, p.43.

23 *Birtsmorton Court as drawn in the early 19th century by Maria Martin. William Huskisson, statesman with the unfortunate distinction of being the first passenger to die in a railway accident, at the 1830 opening of the Liverpool-Manchester railway, was born here in 1770.*

A picture of the chase begins to emerge from the medieval evidence and examination of features still visible in the parishes today. In Longdon, for example, whilst there seems to have been no commercial activity such as that at Upton and Hanley, there was enough money to build a stone church in the 14th century. The parish was subject to serious flooding, much of it being marshland which was not properly drained until the 19th century. Perhaps it was able to produce substantial quantities of reeds and rushes for rush-lights and floor coverings. It may also have offered summer grazing when other parishes suffered from drought, as well as attracting water fowl.* Although in the 12th century Longdon passed to the Folliott family, part of it was sold back to Westminster Abbey in 1397.† Adjacent Castlemorton was known as Morton Folliott because it, too, was owned by that family, which was probably responsible for the small castle built in the 12th century during the turmoil of Stephen's reign.‡ Its site is now unceremoniously known as Castle Tump, south of the church, which itself dates from the 12th century.

Like Castlemorton, Birtsmorton appears to have been part of the manor of Longdon at the time of the Domesday Survey. Both the church and the court probably date from the 14th century, though most of the surviving court building is 15th- and 16th-century. The parish took its name from the Brut family, later passing to the Nanfans, whose chaplain in the early 16th century was Cardinal Wolsey.§

Berrow was part of the manor of Overbury in 1086 and therefore part of the possessions of Worcester Priory. Its church dates from the 12th century. Bromsberrow, in Gloucestershire, declined in value from £8 before the Conquest to £5 after it. Although no mention of a church is made in the Domesday Survey, parts of the church seem to date from the early 13th century and the font is Norman.

*   Mark Bowden, *op.cit.*, p.44.
†   *Victoria County History*, Vol. IV, p.112.
‡   *Victoria County History*, Vol. IV, p.49.
§   *Victoria County History*, Vol. IV, p.31.

Welland was not specifically mentioned in Domesday Book but was probably included as part of the manor of Bredon, owned by the Bishop of Worcester. It certainly appeared as part of Bredon manor in the 1299 Red Book of Worcester, which provides information about the customs, rents and extent of episcopal lands at that time. As we have seen, the bishop was granted the remarkable privilege of clearing over 300 acres in Upper Welland at the end of the 12th century. Welland's watermill was leased in 1299 to William le Donnare, a miller of Bredon, and its 12th-century chapel was promoted to the status of a church by the mid-14th century. By this time the village had presumably grown in importance though, like Berrow and other settlements in the chase, it had no particular claim to fame.

24 & 25 *J. Severn Walker's exterior and interior views of the refectory or guesten hall of Great Malvern Priory. The building was demolished about 1839.*

26 *Dr Nash's representation of Great Malvern Priory church and gatehouse is less fanciful than some portrayals. Encroachment by vegetation, particularly at the east end, was to prove problematic in the early 19th century when many people thought the structure was likely to collapse.*

Considered remote from the temptations of the world, Great Malvern and Little Malvern were attractive to those founding the small Benedictine priories in the late 11th and early 12th centuries. They were not commercially important, though the unsubstantiated legend that St Werstan founded Great Malvern priory after escaping Danish invaders at Deerhurst may have been an attempt to produce a home-grown saint whose shrine would attract lucrative offerings from pilgrims, because the tale concluded with his murder by Welsh invaders. Monasteries were, however, centres of learning, and Great Malvern's second prior, Walcher of Lorraine, was an astronomer and mathematician of considerable renown. He helped to introduce Arabic numbers to the west, thus simplifying life for those who had hitherto used the more complicated Roman system. In 1711 his tomb-stone was rescued from a nearby garden which had once formed part of the cloister, and can now be seen in the north side of St Anne's Chapel. Medieval monastic gardens were renowned for their vegetables and the herbs used in medieval medicine, so presumably both Great Malvern and Little Malvern were blessed with such features. But, of course, the central aim of monastic life was, through seclusion from the world and its temptations, utter devotion to the God whose worship was the foundation of western civilisation, with the papacy in Rome at its heart.

Little Malvern was a very small monastery where, in the late 15th century, such serious lapses occurred that Bishop John Alcock sent the monks to 'worshippfull and holye places', repaired their monastery and allowed them back under threat of 'grevous punyshment' if they misbehaved again.

27   *A 19th-century picture of Mathon Church. The chancel and nave are 12th-century, and the tower is 15th-century. The roof shows the skills of 14th-century craftsmen.*

The existence of a church in each parish underlines the fact that by the later Middle Ages the church wielded enormous power, exercising a stranglehold on thought because few people could read or write. The higher clergy, controlling large estates, enjoyed immense power and privilege, while even the humble parish priest, with the ability to read and write, was held in awe by his illiterate flock, concerned about their destination in the afterlife. Given the lack of interest shown in the church in early 21st-century Britain it is difficult to appreciate the power it exercised in the medieval period. Religion, offering colour and drama, dominated life in a way similar to that in which television dominates life today. Priestly vestments and the stained glass to be found in many churches added to the theatrical effect, increasing the power and interest of the church. Pictures in glass were intended not only to glorify God but to serve as a visual aid to explain the gospel message. Fear of eternal punishment in the fires of hell was a very effective means of bringing to heel anyone who challenged clerical authority. When most homes were simple, small, timber-framed and thatched, the sheer size of church buildings, the holding of services in Latin and the fact that the congregation was not provided with seats all helped to create a sense of awe and humility in the mystified peasant.

Registers of successive bishops show their visitations to various parishes, for example, to dedicate new altars or conduct ordination services. They also intervened in other matters, such as Bishop John Alcock's 1480 reform at Little Malvern Priory or an earlier (1420) bishop's concern

> for a pension yearly to be paid for the sustentation of the vicar of Hanley who has resigned on account of an unfortunate lapse in his left arm and age and illness, to be paid by and at the consent of the prior and convent of Little Malvern, patron of said church.[*]

Although in medieval times, with local stone fairly readily available, many of the chase parishes could afford stone churches, some of the earliest churches in

---

[*]   WRO BA527 899:44/26 (Notes made by the compilers of *The Victoria County History*).

poor woodland parishes were likely to have been timber-framed. Such a church at Newland, built in the 14th century near its boundary with the original parish of Malvern, survived until the mid-19th century when, although in very good condition, it was pulled down to make room for a grand neo-Gothic structure in keeping with the Anglo-Catholic views of its benefactors.

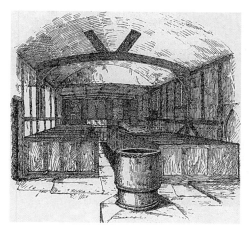 

28 & 29   *J. Severn Walker's architectural sketches of Newland Church in 1863 shortly before it was replaced. In 1855* The Ecclesiologist *stated that the 14th-century church was in such substantial repair that it 'seems likely yet to outlast many fabrics of brick and stone – ostensibly more durable works of the present day.' The fashion for mock Gothic led to its replacement only nine years later.*

30   *The old photograph puts Newland Church in its woodland context – probably there were many other such woodland churches in the extensive forest regions of Worcestershire.*

31   *An early 20th-century picture of Colwall Church with the Church Ale House to the right.*

By the 13th century Mathon had a rabbit warren and a deer park at Farley.[*] In 1287 the Earl of Gloucester accused William Poer of damaging Malvern Chase by making the park and a deer leap, but the bottom must have fallen out of the case when it was established that William's father had made the park and the Earl's father had given him deer to keep in it. Further piquancy comes from the fact that by the time of the accusation most of the deer had been killed by wolves. Such snippets of information indicate the wild nature of the terrain, though the parish could afford a stone church.

The Herefordshire Beacon lies within Colwall, which was a manor belonging to the Bishop of Hereford in the Middle Ages. Lying between the bishop's chase and that of the Earls of Gloucester, Colwall was the scene of boundary disputes and, like Mathon inhabitants, its residents were forbidden in 1540 to 'staff-drive any kind of their cattle into the Chase further than the Shire-ditch after the old' custom.[†] This seems to mean that it was permissible for their animals to wander into the Worcestershire part of the chase, but they must not be driven into it – a nice distinction which must have led to some interesting confrontations. Some people believe that a view of Colwall from the hillside inspired William Langland in his vivid portrayal of medieval life as he wrote about Piers Plowman's vision. Colwall's church seems far from the homes of most of its inhabitants, but this is because much of what we think of as the centre of Colwall was developed in the 19th century. Its old church has Norman and early Gothic features, while its Church Ale House reflects the social life of the later medieval period – a reminder that even in the uncertainties of that time people made the most of opportunities for enjoyment.

---

*   *Victoria County History*, Vol. IV, p.140.
†   Morgan Watkins, *Continuation of Duncumb's History of Herefordshire*, 1902, p.56.

32   *The oldest parts of Leigh Church date from Norman times. Shown here is the 14th-century tower at the west end, with the attached 15th-century porch. Dedicated, like several other churches built on land owned by Pershore Abbey, to King Alfred's grand-daughter St Eadburga, this large stone church reflects the power and wealth of the abbey, which owned the manor of Leigh for several centuries.*

33   *The tithe barn at Leigh, now protected by English Heritage, was restored in 1987-8 under the direction of F.W. Charles, a noted expert on medieval building. The picture shows something of the massive roof structure, the traditional wide doorways to permit entry by wagons, and mill stones at the far end.*

The extensive parish of Leigh, whose most southerly region – usually considered as Howsell and Malvern Link – was part of Malvern Chase, was clearly much more important than some of the other parishes which had land in the chase. From pre-Norman Conquest times the manor of Leigh belonged, like so much in this region, to Pershore Abbey, one of the abbots actually dying there in 1289.[*] Together with Bransford, it seems to have been quite prosperous at the time of the Domesday Survey, when between them they had four mills. When Henry VIII dissolved the monasteries the manor of Leigh was valued at just over £67 and was sold into lay hands. Leigh's 14th-century tithe barn, built for the storage of crops paid as dues to the abbey, is said to be the longest medieval barn and the largest cruck building in the country[†] – an indication of the wealth of its monastic owners and of Leigh's significance in medieval times.

Medieval settlements were much influenced by factors which it may be difficult for us to understand. The life of the medieval peasant was intimately bound up with nature – the seasons and the landscape coloured every aspect of it. Also constrained by the ever present powers of the church and the manorial lord, it was often unpleasant and usually short.

[*]   *Victoria County History*, Vol. IV, p.103.
[†]   Nikolaus Pevsner, *Worcestershire*, 1977, p.212.

VI

Trouble in the Forest

So much has been written about Malvern Chase that it is difficult to separate fact from fiction. There are, as we have seen, the standard horror stories of oral history preserving the largely fictitious notion of mutilating punishments for breaking forest laws anywhere in the land. Locally, the 19th-century rector of Pendock, the Rev. W.S. Symonds, is responsible for much confusion, though his passion for natural history and for local history has endeared him to many. He was very knowledgeable but his novels *Malvern Chase* and *Hanley Castle* were romantic stories which, whilst enthralling his readers, were based only loosely on real events. Getting at the truth of all this is far from easy but there are certain documents which act as signposts to the real facts, though little has been uncovered for the early years of Malvern Forest.

By the second half of the 16th century rather more written material relating to Malvern Chase is available. Much of this was hand-copied into a large bound volume kept in Gloucestershire Record Office. Some was also printed for limited circulation[*] to those interested in the history of the Hornyold family, staunch Roman Catholics who owned large estates centred on Blackmore Park in the heart of Malvern Chase.

John Hornyold acquired Blackmore Park towards the end of the reign of Henry VIII, and immediately challenged chase officials such as John Russell, whom he accused of destroying the deer and damaging the woodland, hedges and ditches. Hornyold himself was accused of coming to Blackmore Park with a gang of others, all armed, to expel Russell, with the result that a riot ensued.[†] It was a foretaste of things to come.

Hornyold expanded his estates, obtaining the manor of Hanley in 1559 from the young Elizabeth I. Growing animosity between him and John Knotsford of Malvern caused him to write to her Lord Treasurer, Burghley, concerning commoners' rights in the Chase. Some researchers have suggested that about 8,000 or 9,000 people enjoyed common rights, but this figure seems too high to be applicable only to Malvern Chase, and perhaps includes adjacent forest land. Copies of State Papers Domestic and the Hornyold family's privately printed document clearly put the number of commoners in Malvern Chase at about 800 or 900, which seems more realistic. It is also commensurate with the population a century later, in 1676, when the church took the Compton census. The 1676

---

[*] J.J. Howard and H. Seymour Hughes, *Genealogical Collections Illustrating the History of Roman Catholic Families of England. Part IV, Hornyold,* 1892.

[†] WRO 527 899:44/26 Notes made by the compilers of the *Victoria County History.*

34 *Nash's 18th-century portrayal of the Hornyold mansion at Blackmore, a Georgian-style house which succeeded the early building and in the 19th century was itself replaced by a Tudor-style mansion.*

churchwardens of Welland parish found 'ye number of male inhabitants to result to 72 from 16 yeares and upward, besides women and children'.[*] At the same time the tiny neighbouring parish of Little Malvern gave its population as 40, presumably also excluding women and children. Such figures suggest a total in all 13 parishes of Malvern Chase, allowing for the more populous nature of Upton, of no more than one thousand men. Probably most had common rights, entitling them to graze sheep and cattle and allow their pigs to forage for acorns and beechnuts.

Hornyold, one of the richer men in the area, wrote with false modesty to Burghley on 5 December 1573 'ffrom my poore howse in Blackemore p'ke' that

> There be comoners within the Chace to the nombre of viij^c or ix^c dwelling within the said Chace and they all p'ceve comen of Herbage and panage throughe thole Chace withoute the extente of nombre and withoute paienge of anythinge.[†]

Hornyold's letter confirms the existence of medieval rights but points out that they were now being abused. He referred to two extensive areas of woodland

[*]   WRO 80/BA2289/21 (vii).
[†]   WRO 714 228.102/1 State Papers Domestic, p.13.

where the commoners had common of estovers, the right to pick up windfall wood for fuel. One was the Earl's Wood, a name sometimes contracted to Therles Wood. The other was Bishop's Wood in neighbouring Welland, part of the land held since before the Norman Conquest by successive bishops of Worcester who had enjoyed hunting there before the Conqueror's afforestation. Within these two extensive woods it was accepted that everyone with common rights could pick up windfall wood, but some were felling trees on a large scale, contrary to forest law. By paying the fine, known as an attachment, for tree felling they were paying far less than the timber was really worth. Hornyold acknowledged that the potters of Hanley paid fees to dig clay for making their pots, bricks and tiles, but

> Comoners haue comen of Estovers in such lardge sorte that eche of them ... do cut downe dailie the great okes and trees ... bestowinge them upon buildinges, ffewell for their howses, and to make malte cley pottes, bricke and tyle, which they convey downe by water to Bristowe, Gloucetor and other places, paieinge for the same trees onelie attachements.[*]

He referred to his own Blackmore Park

> which standeth in the verie harte of Malverne Chace ... and was parcell of the said Manor of Hanley, within which parke there is above three hundrethe acres that in time past was arrable grounde, wherupon certaine of therles ten'ntes did then dwell.[†]

His subsequent purchase of the manor of Hanley gave Hornyold 'of demaines more grounde than anie xl comoners together have', his lands entitling him to common rights, which he exercised. He claimed, however, that he did not fell trees and bemoaned the changed character of the area within the last years as a result of excessive tree felling, encouraged by John Knotsford. If his allegations were true, forest law had been flagrantly broken and only 120 deer remained despite the forest laws designed to protect them. Expressing concern for the future of the chase, he wrote to the Lord Treasurer that there was no forest or chase in the realm

> in so shorte a time so spoiled of woodde and dere as this chace, ffor of one thousande dere Mr Knottesforde hathe not presently lefte Cxx, and where in the first yere of the quenes majesties reigne the grete okes were so thick together that a wayne cold not passe but in certaine places, There is nowe, betwixte oke and oke, tenne score and in some places more & in some places lesse, so that without reformac'on yt cannot contynue above x yeres.

Knotsford, like Hornyold, was a rich and influential man, who had expanded his estates fairly recently. He acquired much of the property of Great Malvern Priory in the 1540s after it was dissolved by Henry VIII. His home, part of the former priory estate, was on the site of the present *Abbey Hotel* and even incorporated part of the monastic church itself. Hornyold claimed that Knotsford was spreading false rumours against him among the locals, complaining to the Lord Treasurer that Knotsford 'hathe sought to deface and bringe me to the speche of the comen people'.

---

[*]   *ibid.* p.14.
[†]   *ibid.*

Hornyold, calling Knotsford a man 'who brawlethe and quarelleth with other men that offend not', clearly loathed him. Without doubt the feeling was reciprocated, especially since Hornyold pressed his case with quite detailed allegations, deploring Knotsford's encouragement of locals – even those with small holdings of only half an acre – to exercise common rights, thereby further depleting the woodland. Although such smallholders were the very people to whom common rights were particularly valuable, Hornyold claimed that Knotsford encouraged abuse of those rights. Commoners, especially from Malvern and Upton, were felling trees on a large or commercial scale. They were driven by two main aims: building and trade. The first meant that 'dailie they builde more and more, with which pollicy to make increase of Rentes', and the second that they were firing kilns to produce 'as miche bricke, tyle, erthen pottes, and malte as thei can possible make, which is grete, Because thei have the trees in maner for nothinge'.

Undoubtedly forest law was being flouted, but some fines were neverthe-less being exacted, apparently to the financial benefit of Knotsford. Hornyold reckoned that in the time of Henry VIII the fines amounted only to just over £4 a year but by the 1570s had increased tenfold to about £40 or £50 a year. Most of this, he claimed, went into the pocket of John Knotsford, who considered himself entitled to them as lord of the manor of Malvern. Knotsford responded that the fines were used to pay the wages of the forest keepers, an explanation that Hornyold robustly challenged. The exact total of fines is not clear – nor is the owner of the pocket into which they fell. But one thing is clear – William the Conqueror's forest was being eaten into by clearance and building on a scale that had never been officially authorised.

Although John Hornyold appears to have died in 1575, and was succeeded by his son Ralph, further documents, dated 15 May 1581, throw light upon the quarrel between the Knotsford and Hornyold families. Knotsford, so bluntly accused by Hornyold, counter-accused the latter of cutting 'downe muche of the Quines Majties wod within Malverne Chace', causing the authorities to demand proof of the Hornyold family's title. This produced a list of statements to prove that the wood was part of the Hornyold manor of Hanley. Firstly, 'therles wod (or the lordes wod), which is part of the manor of Hanley', which John Hornyold had bought from Elizabeth I, contained common land on which the tenants of nine manors had the right to pick up windfall wood (estovers) but not to fell trees. If they felled trees they had to pay fines (attachments), which although John Hornyold 'moight iustlie have' … 'yet he dothe leve them to the quenes majestie'.

Further statements supporting the Hornyold claim, although difficult to fol-low, are instructive as to forest practices in the late 16th century, and may be summarised as follows:

1. The attachments, or fines, which Hornyold claimed to pass on to the queen, were assessed at Hanley Manor courts and at no other manor court. The practice was comparable with the situation in the other great wood, called Bishops Wood, which was part of the manor of Welland. Attachments as-sessed at Welland Manor court were paid to the Bishop of Worcester, who owned the manor. Hornyold claimed that the rules applicable in the Bishop's Wood should be similarly applicable to his own Earl's Wood in Hanley.

2. The 2s. 6d. (12½p) that Hanley potters paid yearly for licence to dig clay was classified as part of the manor rents. It was taken into consideration when the manor of Hanley was valued in 1559 and bought by Hornyold. The lord of the manor of Hanley also received 10 shillings yearly rent from the prior of Malvern for licence to take fuel from the said wood.

3. Lords of the manor of Hanley received eight quarters of oats from the tenants of Baldor (near Barnards Green) and others in return for these tenants being permitted to drive their cattle into Hanley common. The tenants of Hanley drove the common for 'waief and straies', which unclaimed animals were brought to the pound in Hanley.

4. In Blackmore park some 300 acres, formerly arable, bought of diverse commoners, entitled Hornyold to be a commoner.

More specific reasons for Hornyold anger against Knotsford emerged as the latter was accused of felling 600 oaks, worth £300 – a very large amount indeed – without any right to do so. Knotsford appears not to have denied this considerable erosion of the woodland but claimed he was entitled to do this as he had bought the lands of Great Malvern Priory at the time of its dissolution and considered that he had thus inherited the common rights enjoyed by the late prior of Malvern. The Hornyold interpretation was that when the Crown took possession of the priory estates

> the title of a comoner was extinct and yt cold not be revived in Mr Knottesforde by purchacing of the Scite and demaines of the saide Priory.

In any case, according to the Hornyold argument, the prior had only common rights for fuel. But Knotsford had cut down 'the greate okes' for building, to make malt and for other purposes. Hornyold also stated that Knotsford had a great wood, called Thassertes, worth £1,000, which he claimed as part of his purchase of priory property but he never paid for it and it was a special 'thing of ytself'.

Hornyold also alleged that the attachments (fines) which Knotsford collected in the chase really belonged to the queen, from whom he had concealed the fact that she was entitled to over 1,000 marks, the equivalent of several hundred pounds. He claimed that these facts could be proved by presentments made annually to the steward of the manor of Hanley, but Knotsford had taken and withheld these documents. Hornyold believed that these presentments should in the future be handed over to the Exchequer.

Hornyold's accusations were taken seriously, and there is evidence that the more affluent, who grew enough wood on their own land, had not traditionally taken any from the Chase. This left the Chase wood for poorer people and, of course, avoided stripping vegetation which supported the deer. But from the middle of the 16th century they had apparently shown no such restraint and, by building large new houses with newly felled wood, had dramatically challenged the basic principle of forest law which was to refrain from forest clearance. The landscape of Elizabeth I's forest must have been very different from that which William the Conqueror had so briefly enjoyed 500 years earlier. Notwithstanding its almost non-existent punctuation, an 'Advertysmente to … Lord Burleigh grete tresorer of England'* makes it clear that if nothing is done to stop the practices

---

*   WRO 714 228.102/1.

of the last 30 or 40 years, such extensive forest clearance would be disastrous for the poor as well as for the deer:

> The anncient custome was that those fermors and freholders and such as had suffycient of theire owne to burne or imploye other wise growyng on theire owne fermes or tentz did not cut any wood in the Chase but very littell suche as they had not of theire owne grothe and moight be spared oute of the Chase and by meane thereof the Chase contynned faire full of wood and dere until about 30 or fortye years past the saide farmers and ffreholders and other spoylers have solde the woode that grewe on theire ground and by color of theire owne some of the Chase wood, and buylded suche large and costly houses only with the Chase tymber that the saide Chase is made so bare of trees and wood that if present remedy be not had the pore that have no refuge but only theire common in the Chase being fare from any place where any wood is to be bought wilbe utterly undon and all the covert and the Quenes deere utterly spoyled.

By way of remedy for all these ills, it was suggested that central government should act upon the information given about abuse:

> For remedy whereof I think but necessary either by letter or Comyssion sent unto my Lord Busshopp of Worcester to John Russell of Strenesham and Richard Lygon Esqyer especyally And to the residence of the saide benche of Hanley to see the wood kept in state and that suche wood as may be spared be allowed to suche poore men onely as are nether able to buye or have of theire owne growthe so shall the olde good order be revived the poore provided for and the covert and the Quenes deere savyd ...

> Endorsed An information of certen spoiles comitted uppon the Woode in Malverne Chase con. Wigorn with meanes to redress the same.

Unsurprisingly, some details of the claims made by the main protagonists are suspect. John Hornyold, for example, reckoned that the Chase harboured a thousand deer in the 1550s, but the jury responding to Queen Mary Tudor's enquiries in 1558 put the figure at 'six hundred Deare as they do esteeme them'.[*] Even so, whatever the rights and wrongs of the Hornyold and Knotsford statements, by the 1570s forest law had clearly been largely ignored for at least a generation and probably much longer. Nevertheless, John Suffield, keeper of the Bruerne Walk, encompassing Hanley, Upton, Longdon and Castlemorton, was apparently conscientious in trying to carry out his duties. His 'boke for 1576' has survived and sets out the 'tachements paid by men who had fallen wodde within the said chace'. It also included payments of one penny for 'digginge claye in the parish of Hanley' confirming that the pottery industry still provided employment. An intriguing entry shows that one such payment was made by Cale the minstrel.[†]

A perambulation of the Chase was carried out in 1584, presumably in an attempt to tighten up control. Before examining that in detail, it is worth looking at a significant 1581 document. It seems that the complaints were to yield results.

---

[*] WRO BA1751 705:295/2.
[†] WRO. 705:24/360.

VII

Official Concerns

In the event of a scandal which cannot be buried central government often feels a need to flex its muscles so that it appears to be doing something. The complaints made so robustly by John Hornyold seem to have led to some attempts at reform, a response which lends credibility to his claims. The surviving document* detailing steps to be taken has been damaged, several lines of it being totally missing. Fortunately, when intact, it was copied into the large book of records† previously mentioned. Although this copy contains minor errors, the substance of the attempts at reform carried out in 1581 is very clear, and the document reveals what had been happening in the chase over the previous generation or two. Certaine orders were

> made the xvth daye of Maye for the preservacon of the Chase of Malverne by the Jurye whose names do follow.

These jurors were 15 substantial landowners who, by issuing orders set out in 30 clauses, were to end abuses and preserve the Chase. Failure to comply with their orders carried fines ranging from a few shillings to £10 – much above the standard upper limit of £2 fines imposed by local manorial courts.

Numerous orders refer to the protection of young trees and other vegetation:

> In primis that no Commoner within the Chase of Malverne doe cutt or cause to be cutt or cropte anye younge oke within the saide Chase for and to the use of any manner of person beinge under six feete about at fyve feete heighte upon payne of Forfayture for everie tree so cutt or cropped xiijs iiijd.
> Itm that no person shall from henceforth peele anye Hollyes within the saide Chase neither gather or batedowne anye ackorns within the saide Chase upon payne of fforfaiture for everye such offence iijs iiijd
> Itm that no manner of person shall cutt downe or croppe anye named tree upon payne of forfaiture of XLs

The high fine of 40 shillings for damaging a named tree – three times that for damaging young trees – reflects the importance of mature trees which would have yielded valuable timber but were vital in maintaining the forest habitat, and might also have been local landmarks. The authorities clearly accepted that extensive felling in recent years had been to meet not only the need for fuel

---

*   WRO 705:24/352.
†   WRO 714 228.102/1.

but also to satisfy the greed and ambition of men who had been large scale
despoilers of the forest:

> Itm that no manner of person shall from henceforth carrie or cause to be carried
> give deliver conveigh or willinglye suffer to be conveighed out of and from the
> liberties of the Chase anye manner of fuell or tymber whatsoever which hath
> dothe or hereafter shall growe within the saide Chase of Malverne uppon payne
> of forfaiture for everie suche offence V^{li}.
>
> Itm that no commoner haveinge an howse allreddy builded within the liberties of
> the same Chase shall frome henceforth builde or cause to be builded anye cottages
> or dwellinge howses uppon any parte of his grounde with anye of the Chase
> Tymber except the same builded or sett uppe where some Mesne in olde tyme
> hath byn uppon payne of forfeiture for everie such cottage or dwellinge house so
> builte XL^{s}

The fines for these two offences were high, at £5 and £2, indicating the
perception that they seriously damaged the forest. Although the above order
permitted rebuilding on an old inhabited site (mesne), there followed a clear
indication that parts of the wasteland had been newly enclosed to provide sites
for new cottages – possibly on a large scale. Enclosure of common land took it
out of public and into private ownership so those who exercised common rights
naturally objected to the loss of land over which they exercised them. Whilst it
is not clear how long such enclosure had been going on, it was for at least 30
years and probably very much longer.

> Itm that all such cotages and dwellinge howses which have byn builded and set
> uppe within the Circuyte of the Chase and liberties of the same within this xxx^{tie}
> yeares laste paste from henceforth be by this order utterlye discomyned.

Presumably in an attempt to limit the desire for enlarging houses householders were forbidden to take in undertenants. This order is a forerunner of later
legislation to address a major problem that, nationwide, beset parish officials
who had to implement the new 1601 poor law. Parishes, made responsible in
1601 for providing for the poor within their boundaries, did not welcome newcomers who might require assistance from poor rates collected from the pockets
of local residents.

> Itm it is ordered that all such persons dwellinge within the liberties of the Chase
> which have taken anye under tenant or undertenants into his or theire dwellinge
> howses within three yeares last paste shall before the feaste of All Saints next
> comynge remove the same undertenant uppon payne of forfeiture for everie suche
> offence xx^{s}. And that no person shall from henceforth take anye undertenante into
> his or their dwellinge howses other than the faither the Child and the Childe the
> faither for necessities sake uppon lyke payne.

Commercial use of the Chase wood was also to be stopped, an order which
shows that such commercial use included not only standard baking and brewing
but the more specifically local pottery industry, centred on Hanley Castle:

> Itm that no Baker or Brewer which baketh or breweth to sell dwellinge in Upton
> uppon Severne, Wellande, Moretonfollie , Moreton Birte Keiesende Berrow Moche
> Malverne and Little Malverne or in anye of them shall from henceforth use anye
> of the Chase Wodde to Bake or Brewe therewithall for vittaylinge as is abovesayde,
> uppon forfeite for everie tyme so offendinge x^{s}.

Itm that no person or persons usinge the trade or crafte of pottinge makinge of Bricke tyle or anye other earthen stuffe within the liberties of the Chase shall burne or eyle anye of the said potte bricke or tyle or anye other earthen stuffe betwene the feaste of Sainte Andrewe thappostle and St David beinge the firste of Marche uppon payne of everie one soe offendinge to forfeite vj^s viij^d And that they make nomore within the saide tyme upon like payne

Itm that the saide potters and all other makeinge earthen stuffe of what sorte soever it be shall not from henceforth Cutt down anye manner of wodde but Roote, Comynes and other like offell wodde for the ealinge of theire potts bricke or tyle or anye other earthen stuffe shall forfeite for every Wayne lode iij^s iiij^d and for every horse lode vi^d.

Other commercial uses of wood were also banned by an order referring to wood-burning or perhaps charcoal making:

Itm that no comoner or other doe use anye of the Chase wodde to make wodde asshes uppon payne of fforfaiture for every suche offence xl^s

Itm that from henceforth there shalbe no new oven comonlye called yealinge ovens made within the liberties of the Chase of Malverne for the ealinge of bricke tile or anye other earthen stuff uppon payne of forfaiture for every oven soe sett upp xl^s

This was quite a high penalty, as was that for using Chase wood for malt making:

Itm that no comoner within the Chase which doth use comon malte makeinge shall from henceforth burne anye of the Chase wood for that purpose uppon payne of forfeiture of xx^s for every offence.

Pigs were always a problem. Putting rings through their noses reduced the damage they could do when they rooted among rubbish, as they often did in the streets and churchyard of Upton, as well as in the forest:

Itm that no Comynner haveinge swyne goeinge within the Chase shall suffer them to goe unringed from Michaelmas until Sainte Martines daie uppon payne of forfeiture of iiij^d for every Pigge so unringed.

As already indicated, the status of Herefordshire inhabitants in Malvern Chase was rather distinct from that of Worcestershire people, and they were not allowed to drive their animals across the shire ditch. They were also forbidden to:

take or drawe awaye from and out of the hill anye timber or fuell uppon payne of forfaiture for every offence xx^s.

An interesting view appears on the controversial issue of enclosure, which was to be raised on innumerable occasions in the future. Clearly an undefined, but possibly large, amount of enclosure had not only taken place but also had been accepted. This is suggested by orders which do not object to enclosures but do object to the use of chase wood for the purpose of hedging round them:

Itm that no person or persons within the liberties of the Chase shall frome hence-forth Cutt downe or cause to be cutt downe anye thornes or underwodd in the sayde Chase for anye theire severall enclosures uppon payne of forfeiture for every Wayne lode vj^s viij^d And for every draylode iij^s iiij^d

> Itm that no person frome henceforth use anye of the Chase Wodde for stakes for
> theire severall and newe enclosures uppon payne for everie offence iij^s iiij^d

Since a stint had been imposed to specify how many animals could be left to graze by each commoner, penalties were high for exceeding one's own allowance:

> Itm that no Comoner shall frome henceforth foster or beare anye kynde of Cattell
> fraudulently within the Chase otherwise then his owen upon payne of xx^s for every
> beaste so taken And that no Commoner or other shall from henceforth kepe any
> sheepe within the Chase but accordinge to tholde order which is xxx^{tie} at the moste
> for every ploughe lande and for every freeholder x and for every Cottager sixe
> unlesse they kepe them upon the hill upon like payne.
> Itm that no Comoner havinge anye ploughe or teeme shall keepe anye Gottes
> within the Chase of Malverne nor anye other person shall kepe above sixe gotts at
> the most uppon payne of forfeiture for every offence for every gott iij^{s}iiij^d

The practice of tree-grafting was well established, and even the use of fruits such as crab apples was also to be carefully regulated:

> Itm that no person shall henceforth gather any Crabbes within the chase before
> the Nativitie of oure Ladie yearely uppon payne of forfeiture of iij^s iiij^d for every
> offence And that they doe not fall or cutt downe anye crabbe tree/peare tree/or
> whippe croppe otherwise then to graff the same peare or crabbe tree there/uppon
> like paine for every offence.

Concern that wild plants should not be removed by private individuals is not as modern as we might believe:

> Itm that no person shall frome henceforth sell give carie or otherwise conveigh
> out of the Chase and liberties of the same anye Hollies quickesette crabbe trees or
> peare trees stocke which do or shall growe within the said Chase upon paine of
> forfeiture for every suche offence x^s

The particular restrictions on lopping or felling trees which served as special landmarks indicate to us 400 years later which those landmarks were, even if we have difficulty in locating them precisely:

> Itm that no manner of person shall from henceforth fall or croppe or cause to
> be fallen or cropped anye tymber tree or anye other tree for fuell beneath the
> deareleapestile gospell oke or three wayes ende uppon payne of forfeiture for every
> tree so fallen lopped or cropped xx^s
> Itm that no manner of person shall frome henceforth fall or croppe or cause to be
> fallen or cropped any manner of tree or trees within the Compasse of the Cleres
> fawtes and hooke upon paine of every one offendinge to forfeite for every tree so
> fallen or cropped contrarie to this order xx^s

Although no effective policing was in operation, there was a strong warning against people taking the law into their own hands to try to stop illegal practices. The fine for disobeying this order was an astonishing £10. Offences were to be dealt with properly by the chase officials taking their orders from the court at Hanley:

> Itm that no person shall vexe suie or molest any comoner for anye offence done
> or committed within the precincte of the Chase out of the lordes courte of Hanley

being the place accustomed for the redressinge of suche disorders within the saide Chase comitted uppon paine of forfeiture for every suche offence x¹ for everie person so sued vexed or molested.

Obviously the cover of darkness made stealthy night-time pilfering attractive to thieves so orders were issued for appropriate punishment:

Itm it is ordered that no manner of person shall from henceforth cutt anye fuell or anye tymber or suche like before the sonne risinge, after sonne settinge or afternowne upon anye Saturdaie upon paine of forfeiture of his or theire tooles which shalbe soe taken loppinge or fellinge.

Forest officials were reminded where their duty lay and the penalty for failing to carry it out:

Itm that no keper within the Chase shall conceale anye Trespasse or offence done or comitted within the same Chase to him knowen contrary to the order of this courte made for the preservacon of the saide Chase but shall make severall presentments of the same offences by him soe knowen to be done or comitted upon payne of forfeiture for every suche concealment and offence xxˢ
Itm that no person shall cutt or carry anye fuell or tymber uppon anye Courte daie or Lawedaye holden at Handley for the manor and Chase there where the kepers are to make their presentments for any offence done or comitted within the sayde Chase upon payne of forfeiture for every offence vjˢviijᵈ

These records give a good picture of life in the forest in the late 16th century. That such orders were necessary is an indication of the sloppiness which had become a feature of forest law enforcement. Maybe such sloppiness was the norm throughout the history of Malvern Chase, and findings of a much earlier period might have been very similar. It is, however, clear that at least some reform was attempted in the last half of the 16th century, even though the queen herself displayed no interest in hunting here.

The Berington archives in Worcestershire Record Office contain references to threats of violence about this time. In 1600 the Court of Exchequer set up a commission

upon complaint made against divers persons for great spoyles and waste committed in hir majesties wodde within the Chase of Malverne.*

Six years later it is clear that problems continued since correspondence referred to the threat that some forest inhabitants 'would assemble multitudes of … unrulye persons … and … Cutt downe and dystroye the woode.'†

Quarter Sessions papers for the end of the 16th and the first half of the 17th centuries provide evidence that the justices of the peace were required to deal with a number of matters which would presumably once have been dealt with by the manorial court at Hanley. For example, between 1591 and 1643 there were in the county 63 cases of sheep-stealing – usually not on a large scale. The chase parishes of Hanley Castle, Birtsmorton and Upton accounted for ten of these cases, leading J.W. Willis Bund,‡ in editing the papers, to conclude that these parishes 'seem to have been the great home of sheep stealing' – rather a harsh judgement.

---

*   WRO 705:24/374.
†   WRO 705:24/378.
‡   J.W. Willis Bund, *Worcestershire County Records, Calendar of Quarter Sessions Papers*, p.lxiv.

Willis Bund also examined offences against game,[*] which involved the use of 'cross bows, bows and arrows, hawks, spaniels and greyhounds' but these cases heard by the justices were across the county as a whole, not simply in the Malvern Chase region. Just outside the boundaries of Malvern Chase in 1611 a man at Ripple was indicted for keeping a greyhound and hunting hares and rabbits with it in a field at Queenhill but the case was not proved. In 1614, however, 'a true Bill' – meaning that there was good evidence – indicted John Hill and William Staunton both of Upton 'for killing a sore deer in the King's Chase called Malvern Chase'. These two were apparently quite respectable, Hill being described as a gentleman and Staunton as a cooper. The case also indicates that there must still have been deer in the chase in the early 17th century, even though John Hornyold claimed in 1573 that there were only 120 left. A case in 1608 also indicates some attempt still being made to protect the vert, for

> John Cope the younger of Berrow, husbandman, and William Lambert and Silvester Powle had to appear to answer for cutting down the king's hollies and covert in the Chace of Malvern being contrary to the ancient custom and order of the said chace.[†]

In 1614 John Kennard, a farmer of Powick, was indicted

> For that he did discharge a piece or gun charged with powder and hail shot at two partridges and the same two partridges then and there with the said gun and shot did kill. A true Bill.[‡]

Willis Bund made another of his rather broad judgements suggesting that the inhabitants of Longdon 'in Malvern Chace' … 'like the inhabitants of Feckenham, seem to have been very rough'.[§] There may, however, have been more substance so far as Longdon is concerned if we are to judge by cases in the period 1614-1625. In 1617 Constable William Jefferies' petition[¶] alerted the justices to behaviour all too well known to modern police in town centres:

> Shewing that the inhabitants and youth of Longdon have every year upon the Sabbath day in the summer time used to sport themselves with May games mor- rices and dancing by reason whereof many rude ruffians and drunken companions have come to there from other towns adjoining to the said sports and have made much quarrelling ready to murder one another. As upon a Sabbath day 1614 some of Forthampton's men coming to the said sports made an affray there and gave one a broken head and upon a Sabbath day 1615 some of Eldersfield's men coming to the said sports made an affray upon the Smith's man of Longdon … the principal actor in the last mentioned affray was one Sandys of Eldersfield who has since cut off his neighbour's arm for doing the office of Constable upon him a little before.

The early 17th century was a time of fierce debate as to what activities were proper on Sundays, the Puritans being hostile to morris dancing even after religious duty had been observed by attendance at church services. To

---

[*] J.W. Willis Bund, *Worcestershire County Records, Calendar of Quarter Sessions Papers*, p.lxix.
[†] *ibid.*, p.110.
[‡] *ibid.*, p.195.
[§] *ibid.*, p. cxl.
[¶] *ibid.*, p.254.

indulge in such merriment during the time that church services were being held was even more controversial. In 1615 when fun and games were stopped during evening service in Longdon some of the young revellers got revenge by forcing a 'poor woman' ... 'and poor boy' to interrupt the service so that 'the whole congregation' was 'much disturbed'. In 1617 the Constable, 'your poor petitioner', tried

> peaceably to take the minstrel there playing and to punish him upon the Statute against rogues. Thereupon one of the dancing company strake up your petitioner's heels and said he would break your petitioner's neck down the stairs there if he departed not from them and let them alone, whereupon your petitioner being much terrified by them departed and afterwards many other abuses were committed that year by the said company too long here to relate unto you.

Possibly the petitioning constable was being officious, but nevertheless he was clearly trying to carry out his duty of enforcing the law as it then stood. Throughout the country law and order was supposed to be kept by parish constables or tithingmen, who were usually appointed annually. They had to 'keep watch and ward' to try to ensure that no breach of the peace occurred and that law-breakers were arrested. Suspects might be put in the stocks, confined in a lock-up or even in the constable's home until brought before the magistrates[*] – clearly, as the above extract shows, a potentially dangerous course of action. It was actually quite common for constables to try to avoid confrontation so the Longdon episode raises some interesting questions about the personalities involved.

Morris dancing did not appear so innocent a pastime as it does today, and the magistrates seemed ineffectual, ordering Sandys of Eldersfield to be of good behaviour and requiring constables to bring before the magistrate 'all morrice dancers who dance in time of divine service unlawful games'.

In 1625 'John Wrenford of Longdon, Gentleman' petitioned[†] the Justices of the Peace because

> David Powell, servant to Nicholas Turett, Clerk ... bears Wrenford and most of his family an inveterate hate and malice and would have fought with him when he was his servant. Some 7 or 8 swine of Wrenford lately died and when flayed the flesh appeared black and Powell has been seen to beat them with a staff and throw them over Turett's hedges. That he hurt two of Wrenford's cart horses so they could not work during harvest that some of Wrenford's horses and cattle got on Turett's ground because his fences were bad and Powell beat them unmercifully and said 'by God's wounds he would beat Wrenford's servants worse.'

In 1608 Henry Dingley of Hanley Castle appealed[‡] to the magistrates to

> call on the Churchwardens and Constables of Hanley Castle to lay open and prevent the great abuses done there on Sabbath days and especially the great riot and unlawful assembly on Sunday last being Whit Sunday by forty persons at least many of them being recusants who daily increase in the said parish.

Recusants were at one end of the religious spectrum and puritans at the other. Recusants risked defying the law to continue worshipping according to Roman

---

[*] Keith Wrightson, *English Society 1580-1680*, 1982, p.158.
[†] J.W. Willis Bund, *op.cit.*, p.399.
[‡] *ibid.*, p.115.

Catholic rites. There were many of them in this region, safe in the protection of rich and influential families such as the Hornyolds of Hanley Castle. It is not clear at which end of the religious spectrum William Staunton stood when in 1620 he was accused of 'opprobious words against the Reverend Father in God, the Lord Bishop of Worcester'.

In 1633 there was another 'riot committed at Hanley Castell', which may well have been connected with the proposals to disafforest the chase, as described in a later chapter.

Many cases of disturbing the peace involved upsets between neighbours or between husbands and wives, such as a Castlemorton couple in 1633. He was accused of abusing her but 'they are since reconciled'. Some things never change. Similarly, in 1607, 'the evil behaviour of John Baskerville of Much Malvern, Weaver' shows that human nature changes little over the centuries.[*]

> He is a common frequenter of alehouses in the village where he dwelleth, spending usually 3 or 4 hours there in a day, contrary to the laws. He is a common receiver of evil company entertaining in his house strangers of evil conversation and suffering them to have chamber in his house.

A search warrant led to an unpleasant scene in which Baskerville threatened the officer that 'if he had not the warrant he would have kicked him down the stairs'. Meanwhile, his wife and children were brought before the magistrate for

> Abusing his neighbour … and killing her rabbits. She has offered to give him a couple or so of conies for himself if he would make his children forbear from stealing the rabbits.

An unusual and sad case occurred in 1607, when a petition[†] was made to the magistrates by William Holland of Castlemorton,

> who served in the Queen's wars in Ireland where he hath gotten many incurable distempers yet he is not able to [earn] his livinge which before this he hath done. He hath lately been visited with more sickness to the utter undoing of himself his wife and their small children.

Extreme poverty – and surely some degree of officiousness – is indicated in another petition brought in 1617[‡] by William Dench, a very poor Longdon labourer with a wife and seven small children. For five years, without licence from the lord of the manor or from magistrates, but with the permission of the churchwardens and overseers of Longdon,

> he dwelt in a Sheepcot given to him and his family by William Parsons of Longdon, Yeoman, which Sheepcot stands on the freehold of the said William Parsons and not on the waste or common.

But officialdom intervened and

> he has been indicted and tried for an outlawry prays the King's Majesty's pardon in respect of the charges and forfeitures he has incurred.

---

* J.W. Willis Bund, *op.cit.*, p.106.
† *ibid.*, p.105.
‡ *ibid.*, p.252.

A law passed during the reign of Elizabeth had made it an offence to let a cottage with less than four acres of land – an attempt to make rural inhabitants economically independent. Several indictments were made against people in and around Malvern Chase over this matter, such as 'John Robyns of Great Malvern for not laying 4 acres of land to his cottage at Malvern Lynk'. This was a fairly common offence, mentioned also at Queenhill and at Inkberrow.

A new form of providing for the poor had been established in 1601. This Elizabethan poor law became the basis for poor relief for the next 233 years. Making each parish responsible for the relief of paupers within its boundaries, it was modified from time to time as the authorities and the poor pitted their wits against each other. In 1605 a labourer and his wife, Robert and Ann Palmer of Great Malvern, were indicted for wandering off and begging at Great Witley but few such cases are recorded for this period.

As well as many little tracks, numerous more major roads ran through the chase parishes. Although they were part of main routes between parishes and the larger towns such as Worcester and Pershore, they were of very poor quality until well into the 18th century. Although the Romans had been renowned for the quality of their roads, little had been done for road-building since their departure in the fourth century. Road repairs had become the responsibility of parishes, none of which showed any enthusiasm for the task. Only the hardiest souls travelled in winter when, in an effort to avoid getting bogged down in mud, travellers took to the edge of the road, making many of them remarkably wide. Even summer travel presented serious hazards when a horse-drawn vehicle might find progress difficult or even turn over in dried-out ruts. Parishes were largely self-sufficient and, given the inconvenience and dangers of long-distance travel, there was little inducement to any except the more adventurous to undertake any journey unless it was really necessary. There was no real motivation for parishes to repair roads since they derived little benefit from the task and saw no point in exerting themselves in order to make life more convenient for a few travellers from foreign parts of the country. In 1633, however, there was a concerted effort by magistrates to improve the condition of county roads by requiring parishes to carry out statutory repairs. Papers have survived to show that, of the chase parishes, Upton, Castlemorton, Welland, Hanley Castle and Birtsmorton were all told to do so.

In fact a more effective national system was needed. It was unrealistic to expect that good roads could be provided by unwilling and unpaid amateurs using any material that came to hand – particularly since they were supervised by an equally unwilling, unpaid and untrained surveyor of the highways. This was the important title given to the unfortunate householder whose turn it was to take on this thankless task.

Things were to change when the idea of turnpike roads caught on at the end of the 17th century, though there were undoubtedly still problems. One of the earliest turnpike trusts was that based on Ledbury as a result of the Ledbury Turnpike Act of 1721. Many people resented the imposition of tolls on road users, and Ledbury experienced a serious riot in 1735. Nevertheless, a turnpike trust based on Upton was set up by an Act of 1752 to administer the main roads leading from Upton. Largely based on existing old roads, these roads improved communication between parishes which had once been in the forest and linked up with roads built by other trusts towards towns such as Worcester,

35   *The old toll cottage on the A449, near the bottom of the Herefordshire Beacon. Now uncomfortably close to a road bearing considerable modern traffic, it would once have been conveniently situated for easy collection of tolls from drivers of horse-drawn vehicles.*

Hereford and Gloucester. The roads to Tirley (now the B4211), towards Colwall and Ledbury (now the A4104), towards Worcester (now the B4211) and through Roberts End in Hanley Castle towards Malvern (now the B4209) all came under the control of Upton Turnpike Trust. Such trusts were empowered to charge tolls, scaled according to the amount of damage the user would cause to the road, and use the proceeds to keep the roads in repair. This was not quite as good as it sounds, since road repair came lower in the order of priority than defraying the expenses of getting the Act passed and paying for the erection of gates and tollhouses. At last, however, some professionalism was creeping into road-building. But as late as 1827 the young Rev. Henry Fothergill, who had led a service at Longdon and was returning to his home on the Upton-Hanley road, met his death because of the terrible state of the road on that December night.*
He drowned when, on the flooded road near his home, his horse stumbled into a disused sawpit about which there had been complaints as long ago as 1660, as recorded in Upton manorial court presentments.

Today it is possible to see evidence of the turnpike era in the still fairly common mile-stones erected by the trusts. More visible but less common survivals are the tollhouses with their characteristic frontages allowing the gatekeeper to stay inside his house from which the angled side windows enabled him to keep an eye open for traffic in both directions.

---

*   There is a memorial tablet, with appropriate biblical quotation, in Castlemorton Church.

VIII

Duty and Pleasure –
a Perambulation

In 1584 a forest official who took part in a perambulation of Malvern Chase recorded 'this note for my owne memorye even as I executed hitt'. Henry Dingley of Hanley Castle would probably be very surprised to find that, more than 400 years later, his account* still attracts attention, showing the humour and fun when a happy band of officials spent a pleasant couple of days riding through the locality trying to ensure that forest law was properly observed. The fact that they were not entirely sure what the task entailed seems to have added to their enjoyment. The record gives some pointers – but no precision – as to the boundaries of Malvern Chase and drives home the point that land-owners could not do whatever they liked with land over which somebody else had hunting rights. There is no indication as to when the last perambulation had taken place. It seems very likely that 1584 saw the first perambulation in many years: perhaps it occurred as the result of the Hornyold/Knotsford quarrel, which churned up so much ill-feeling and led to a tightening up of control by central government. Dingley's six-page document is a homely account which paints a realistic account of what lay beneath the official requirements of forest law.

Henry Dingley, having been alerted 'ffirste in the nighte I beinge in my bedd', was to set off with ten other men, all suitably equipped, meeting early next day

> by an hower set downe ... in Northend greene at the crosse there, A horsbacke with spures upon theire heeles, A sworde girte to theire loynes, A horne aboute theire necke from thense to goe and viewe the lymites and p'cincte of the Chace of Malverne ... and to make presentment thereof at the nexte courte holden for the manor of Hanley Castell.

From the cross in Northend Green they rode to

> the Clyfhey wod yeate and there we did blowe our hornes and furth of the wodd came one Buckwell, a keeper who demaunded of us what wee did lacke: And wee inquiringe of him what he was (thoughe wee did knowe him before) receaved of him aunswere he was the sworne keeper of the linke and Clyfhey wodd; where upon wee required him to shewe us his walke.

In the hierarchy of forest officials Buckwell was relatively lowly – one of the subordinate keepers responsible for their own patch of forest, known as a walk. Buckwell's walk took them as far as Clevelode and Pixham ferry, passing by

---

* WRO BA1751 705:295/2.

36 *J. Oldmeadow's romanticised 1860 portrayal of Pickersleigh House, where North End Lane meets Pickersleigh Road.*

'a water-course not kepte so that the highwaye was surrounded therebye. The owner of this water course wee amerced'. Amercements were the fines imposed by manorial courts, so Dingley and his colleagues did not take the fine then and there, but reported the offence to the court officials, in whose mercy the offender was considered to be.

The old question of the boundaries of the chase is raised, for the perambulation indicates that at this time it extended into Powick. The riders imposed a surprisingly high fine of 40 shillings (£2) when the Powick residents failed to give them the breakfast they had anticipated:

> at the foote of the old hils wee sent the footeman Richard Brawlarde unto the manor of the parsonage of Powicke to advyse the owners and inhabiters therof that wee wold ride thither to brekfaste willinge them ... to provide us meate and provender for our horses: But ... we failed of our Breckfast whereupon wee amersed the owner xlˢ. He paide every pennye.

After this disappointment there was an enjoyable little game to initiate new participants in the perambulation:

> wee came at the lengthe unto a greene cauled Hallington greene ... at this place the viriders that never did ryde before shoulde be made knighte with a naked sworde clapped over the shoulder of which number I beinge one escaped by the swifte runninge off my horse (as lawfull was for mee to dooe)

Forest law forbade the keeping of dogs that had not been hombled, which means that they had had claws removed to try to prevent their savaging deer. It was this concern for the protection of the deer that caused large dogs (*above the bignes*) to be illegal. In theory inspection of dogs should have been carried out twice every seven years.

The riders divided into two groups, excitedly employing what they obviously considered rather a cunning trick to ensure that dogs would be likely to betray their presence by howling:

> the on halfe towards Bransfords Bridge and thother towards Howsewell and pointinge to meete at the overende of the lincke greene we viewed howses ... for dogge water courses and all this waye wee did blowe hornes and hearing doggs

howle wente into the howses to see them and amersed the owners of them that were to bigge and commaunded those suspected to be brought to Hanley to the nexte corte.

A stone which may still be seen in St Matthias Churchyard, Malvern Link, is mentioned in the next extract from the perambulation: when the riders met together

> againe in the lincke greene Buckwell brought us unto a greate stone in a tufte of bushes and said here endethe my walke of the lyncke and Clifhey wodd. Then wee did blow our hornes and furth of a bushe came unto us Francis Browne.

Francis Browne was to show them his walk and, perhaps even more interestingly, took them into Great Malvern, where they probably rode through the Abbey Gateway (more properly called the Priory Gatehouse)

> unto the Abbey Howse to wch place wee had sent Richard Braularde ye footeman before to shewe our cuminge and to have our dinner provided: which was p'formed by old Mr John Knottesforde who tolde us of many thinge wee hadd to dooe in our ridinge: wch wee observed.

37 & 38 *Maria Martin's early 19th-century sketches of the front and rear of the Abbey House. John Knotsford, who quarrelled with John Hornyold and who advised the participants in the 1584 perambulation of the chase, lived on this site which had been within the priory estate. Note the building between the main house and the so-called Abbey Gateway. (Malvern Priory never achieved the independent status of an abbey, and the 'gateway' was actually a gatehouse.) The buildings were much altered between the 16th and 19th centuries. The gatehouse was extended in the late 16th century (about the time of the perambulation), the original gate-posts with their hinge marks still being visible under the archway. These pictures indicate something of the losses incurred by 19th-century development of the former monastic estate.*

This vision of officials carefully attending to the words of knowledgeable old John Knotsford is rather different from that portrayed in the letters of John Hornyold who had so heartily disliked him and complained of his flagrant disregard for the future of the forest. Were Hornyold's accusations well-founded or was Knotsford trying to ingratiate himself now that the game seemed to be up?

After dinner at Knotsford's Abbey House they continued their inspection of this walk and

> nighte approchinge wee devided ourselves againe ... and sume off us went downe Balnors greene and sume Shrewes greene. Heare wee viewed a trough with a hole in hit cauled the Stocke and lock and wee amersed the keeper of the stock bycause the hole hadd not a pin or a wedge in hit cauled the locke this locke turneth the water towe ways.

Having thus inspected Barnards Green and Sherrards Green, they met together again, going down to Guarlford Court where another culinary disappointment awaited them that night, though no fine was imposed:

> The said keeper brought us unto Garlefords Courte where wee should have had our supper: but many of the viryders being alied unto Mr Wheler and his father then lately dead wee spared him upon his entreatye that hee knew not the custome.

This marked the end of the first day of the perambulation and some of the riders had finished their duty. Others were required to continue the next day, depending on the terms by which they held land 'for sume holde by one dayes ridinge and sume by towe dayes as they saye'.

The second day they met 'at the Sweet Oacke', mentioned in early documents as a place of execution. On a map of 1628 (see pp. 74-5) 'swete oke' is marked near 'Moorton Greene' in Castlemorton but another 'swete oke' appears very clearly near the present Hanley Swan cross-roads. The latter seems the more likely meeting place, as they first

> rode to a howse bulded neare Hanley Hall hedge to viewe the incrochment theare and so over the brooke by the hedges to Badgers howse of Tyre Hill where we viewed finding incrochments and hedges of unlegal assyes And wee amersed Badger for the same.

The Badger family lived at Tyre Hill for generations but clearly they were not to be allowed to get away with these two quite serious breaches of forest law. The encroachments meant that land had been taken out of the common land in an attempt to add it to their private property. The matter of the hedges may have been regarded as even more serious, for hedges in the forest were to be of a height that would not stop the deer from getting in among the crops. As we saw in the chapter on medieval forest life, this requirement to keep hedges low must have been one of the hardest burdens for forest inhabitants to bear. The riders were equipped with 'A mesure ... of the lengthe of towe foote and a halfe which wee mesured the hedges wh all as wee did passe this second daye'. According to the 18th-century historian Nash,

> one of the ... verderers shall stand by the hedge, and put the staff over into the ground, holding the same in his hand; and if the highest part of the hedge be

higher than his arm-pit, then the owner thereof shall be punished by amerciament set and viewed by the conscience of the said viewers.

Dingley's record is not always easy to follow, but on the second day they rode in a southerly direction from Hanley through Welland and Castlemorton to Combe Green:

ffrom Gilfild Lane ende and the Quabbes wee rode straighte unto the Garret heade where wee viewed the Stank and the bridges and waies there ... wee came ... to the Combe greene and so a longe the wode stille as the same lieth. In following our journey wee came to the Berrowe Courte and to divers howses theare at one howse nere Mr Nanfans wherin one morley dwelled.

Eventually they reached the edge of the chase, Dingley mentioning place names which are still familiar after the passing of over 400 years. They saw

Charmill Poole (wch is now a meadowe but in tymes past was a mill powde as apereth by the stanke.) A littell on this side the poole groweth a greate oake cauled the white leved oake bycause he bereth white leaves. ffrom Charmill poole we returned backe by Keyse ende and so alonge the Headewaye unto lyttell malverne where is the place wee should have our dinner for that daye and so wee had of Mr Jhon Russell and going from him wee followed the hedges and so came home.

The numerous fines, or amercements, produced by the perambulation yielded an exceptional amount of money at the next manor court held at Hanley:

The nexte courte after our ridinge was a great daye of Aparance of people by reson of the number of dogge above the Bignes and other offence found in the same ridinge whereby I have harde yt was worth in Amercements neare handre twenty powndes.

As well as problems with dogs, many of the offences were 'unlawfull hedges ... I having the measure of ij fote and a halfe putt mye arme over could not reche the grounde from my arme pitt with the mesure in my hande.' Fines were levied on men in Great Malvern, Little Malvern, Welland, Berrow, Castlemorton, Powick, Clevelode, Bransford, Leigh and Newland – another pointer to the extent of the Chase.

This record of the 1584 perambulation is very valuable, giving detail not available from any other source. Its rarity poses several questions. Was this perambulation the only one to take place? Or did they occur quite often but lacked a Dingley to record them? Have other such records been made, but later destroyed or lost? Whilst no definitive answers can be given, it is probably realistic, given other revelations of obvious laxity in the 16th century, to assume that perambulations hardly ever took place. The light-hearted tone of Dingley's account possibly stemmed from his amused appreciation of being a part of the action aimed at satisfying authorities who, having been alerted by the Hornyold/Knotsford correspondence to potential problems, had started asking awkward questions. Many more questions were to follow.

IX

Sixteenth-century Questions
and Answers

S uccessive chief foresters, who headed the hierarchy of officials enforcing forest law, lived in Hanley. There is still a Hanley Hall on the site mentioned by Habington in Gilbert's End but we cannot know for certain that forest offenders were tried at this site. John Noake, a prolific 19th-century writer on Worcestershire, referred in his *Guide to Worcestershire* to a panelled room in Hanley Hall, claiming that it was once a larger court room to which forest offenders were brought for trial. Noake had made some investigation of original documents but also relied on hearsay so is not entirely reliable. Perhaps in the forest's early days trials did take place at the Hanley Hall site but it seems very likely that, with the building of King John's castle in the early 13th century, trials took place in or near the castle. Nash considered that the court site was close to St Mary's parish church:

> Here were held the sessions for tryal of offences committed in the forest, the room of the meeting was where the school-house now is.

Probably courts had been held at various sites, including Hanley Hall and in or near the castle, at various times. Yet another possible site is the present Glebe Cottage, sometimes referred to as Keeper's Cottage, and having at different times belonged to the church and the trustees of the school which is of medieval foundation.

We should not be too surprised that there is so much uncertainty today about the precise practices and methods of law enforcement in the medieval chase. Such ignorance seems also to have prevailed in the late 16th century. In June 1589, five years after Dingley's perambulation, five inhabitants of Hanley Castle, together with four from Great Malvern, two from Little Malvern and one from Castlemorton were questioned as to how forest law had operated in years gone by, and their replies were written down. This is a strong indication not only that medieval practice had never been properly documented but also that it had not been properly implemented for many years. The authorities were now concerned to sort things out. When Nash[*] produced in the late 18th century his magnificent *Collections for a history of the County of Worcestershire* he included these 1589 findings which, though limited in their scope, form an important basis for understanding how some aspects of forest law had been implemented for several generations.

---

* See Chapter III.

The inquiry, carried out on instructions from the court of Queen Elizabeth I, was led by Sir John Russell, the chief forester. The record of proceedings was signed by him and by two other local dignitaries, Thomas Willoughby and Francis Kettilby, both of whom were probably magistrates. The 12 men who made statements in reply to official questions came from varying levels of society, and some would have been in awe of such important men. The following is a summary of the men and their depositions.

1. Henry Dingley of Hanley, aged 40, who, as an official rider, claimed that he inspected as far as Powick Bridge and Bransford, including the Sweet Oaks at Welland. All these parishes, with others, were in the Chase. The record of his riding is still, as we have seen, in existence.

2. John Browne, alias Glover, of Malvern Magna, keeper of the Link and Cliffey walk, 74, had known the chase for 60 years. He believed it encompassed Hanley Castle, part of Upton, Welland, part of Longdon, Castlemorton, Birtsmorton, Berrow, Bromesberrow, Little Malvern, Great Malvern, part of Leigh called Hawswell, Mathon and Collow (Colwall) in Herefordshire. These 13 parishes feature in the statements of other 1589 witnesses and also in 17th-century documents. Browne gave details of a quaint custom alluded to in other places about the power of a keeper if he should meet any Hanley Castle inhabitant guilty of trying to take home on a wagon wood which he had illegally felled. The culprit could be fined if the keeper could put his bow between the man's gateway and the leading horse or ox drawing the cart. If

> the said keeper ... can put his bow before his horse's or oxe's head ere he cometh within his gate; that then the said keeper ... may attach his wood, and make him pay his fine for the said trespass done.

As a keeper Browne claimed to have done this very thing himself, taking the wood for himself and making sure that the court fined the man who had failed to get his illegally acquired spoils safely back home. He had to attend the court in Hanley and 'yield his account and books of the trespasses and attachments'. For 60 years he had known the custom that deer must not be killed by the inhabitants of Hanley Castle, even if they strayed into the manor. No deer could be forced out of Hanley back into the chase unless the removal was performed by the official keepers.

3. John Williams of Hanley Castle, aged about 93, had known the chase for 60 years, and agreed with John Browne over numerous matters: the list of parishes comprising the chase, the right of Hanley inhabitants to pick up windfall wood and the illegality of cutting down wood or attempting to remove deer.

4. Thomas Powell, bondman of Hanley Castle, aged about 70, had known the chase for 60 years and believed the whole of Hanley Castle was within its boundaries, as well as the Cliffy Wood and the Link Wood, which had had keepers. He thought that no ground in Hanley Castle was 'free from depasturing and feeding of the said deer but only Blackmore Park, which is a park enclosed'.

5. Edward Baxter of Great Malvern, aged about 66 had known the chase for 50 years. He thought it extended to Upton Bridge and further, as Dingley had said, suggesting that Powick and Bransford were widely thought to be included. It was not lawful for Hanley inhabitants to disturb deer feeding on their land but the keepers could go anywhere in Hanley. He had heard that Benchers used to sit at Hanley Church for reformation of disorders of the said chase.

6. William Knight, of Great Malvern, aged about 79, had known the chase for 70 years and agreed with what earlier deponents had said.

7. Richard Tipping, a glover of Great Malvern, aged about 68, had known the chase for about 60 years. He agreed with earlier deponents and added to Baxter's comment on Benchers that there

> were certain gentlemen called Benchers, which were accustomed to sit at Hanley Church for reformation of disorders of the said chase, as this deponent hath heard; and more he knoweth not.

Clearly he was doing his best but there is a sense of uncertainty in his testimony, though his comment on the benchers was picked up by the next witness.

8. John Simmonds, a yeoman farmer of Hanley Castle, aged about 60, had known the chase for 50 years. He said it was lawful for Hanley inhabitants to be attached if the keeper could set his bow before his ox's or horse's head, as John Browne had said. He also knew about Tipping's gentlemen Benchers who used to sit at 'the church house of Hanley'. There were keepers appointed by the chief forester in the Cliffey and the Link. Deer could go anywhere in Hanley and inhabitants must not kill them, though keepers could drive them off.

9. Thomas Mann, husbandman of Little Malvern, aged about 70, had known the chase for 50 years and agreed with the others. He added that Sir John Russell was the chief forester and received one third of the value of attachments, the other two-thirds going 'to the queen's majesty'.

10. John Burford, husbandman of Little Malvern, aged about 60, had known the chase for 50 years. He agreed with earlier witnesses.

11. John Bray, husbandman of Castlemorton, aged about 60, had known the chase for about 50 years. He stated that two-thirds of forest fines went to the queen and one third to Sir John Russell, chief forester. If deer went into Hanley it was not lawful for inhabitants to hurt, kill or destroy them.

12. Richard Edge, yeoman of Hanley Castle, aged about 50, had known the chase for 30 years and agreed with the evidence of other witnesses. He believed the chase stretched 'from the Shire Ditch on the top of Malvern-hill unto the middle of the channel of Severn'.

The 12 witnesses were asked five main questions (*interrogatories*), some with subsidiary questions. Their replies – and we should perhaps bear in mind that they were mostly elderly men unused to legal probing – were sometimes rather general, answers to one question overlapping the answers to others. Clearly they listened to what each other had to say, and when any one of them added some new snippet of information it triggered a reaction in those who came after to add a comment on the new information. None of the earlier witnesses mentioned, for example, the gentlemen benchers or who benefited from the fines. After Baxter mentioned the benchers so did Tipping and Simmonds. Similarly, after Mann mentioned the beneficiaries of the fines so did Bray and Edge.

The record of the proceedings gives ample evidence not only of the total ignorance of officialdom as to the laws theoretically applied to the chase but also a naivety in their methods of seeking to ascertain them. From the witness replies, it is clear that the officials sought and recorded any crumb of information, their original questions seeking the most basic facts. The results of each section in the inquiry may be summarised as follows:

1. *What is your name, age and place of residence? How long have you known Malvern Chase?*

   This ascertained the credentials of the witnesses who were clearly hand-picked for their extensive experience and knowledge. The youngest was Henry Dingley who had recorded his perambulation of the chase and was now 40 years old, while the oldest, aged 93, had known the chase for 60 years. The record period of familiarity with the chase was the 70 years claimed by 79 year old William Knight of Great Malvern. Some had official positions in the chase or connections with an officer. Dingley was a rider, Browne was a keeper and Edge had 'heard his father report, being a very old and ancient keeper'.

2. *What do you believe to be the boundaries of the chase?*

   This was to ascertain the extent of the chase but answers may not have been complete. John Browne listed 13 constituent parishes with which another three witnesses agreed. But other places were mentioned by some deponents whilst others may also have been in the chase but not mentioned by the witnesses, some of whom were quite vague in their answers.

3. *What is the status of Hanley Castle? What rights do its inhabitants have in the chase?*

   Answers relating to Hanley Castle and its inhabitants indicate wide agreement that it was a special part of Malvern Chase and that its inhabitants could pick up windfall wood (common of estovers) but could be fined by chase officials if they actually felled wood and carried it off.

4. *Do the Cliffey and Link woods have keepers? Can Hanley Castle residents cut down wood in them?*

   There was wide agreement about the appointment by the chief forester of keepers for the Cliffey and Link woods. Richard Edge, who had known the chase for 30 years said that his father, as a keeper in the Cliffey wood, had taken attachments there. Richard Tipping and several others confirmed that keepers could take attachments. Thomas Mann and John Burford offered the further detail that two-thirds of such fines went to the queen and one third to the chief forester. This makes it clear that it was in the interests of the chief forester to appoint men who would perform their duties vigilantly and enable prosecutions to be made. Two of the witnesses referred to the benchers who sat at or near Hanley Church, 'for reformation of disorders of the chase'. Both witnesses claimed to know little about the benchers, who seem no longer to have been in existence by 1589. Indeed several of the customs of the chase seem by then to have been but distant memories.

5. *What happens if deer go into the manor of Hanley Castle?*
    It was generally agreed that deer were free to wander and graze wherever
    they wished in the chase, including in Hanley, except for that part of Hanley
    known as Blackmore 'which is a park enclosed'. As was the case in other
    parts of the chase, residents were not allowed to drive off the deer – which
    prohibition pinpoints the greatest problem faced by chase inhabitants strug-
    gling to farm. It was, however, legal for the keepers to enter 'without any
    let or trespass' upon any part of Hanley to drive out deer.

A careless attitude to forest administration clearly prevailed in the later
Middle Ages and the early 16th century. This led to certain benefits for modern
enquirers because it created a situation which encouraged late 16th-century
officials to pose exactly the sort of questions which later historians would wish
to have answered.

Within 50 years much more information was to emerge, as 17th-century parliaments challenged the Stuart kings who proclaimed belief in their divine right
to rule. The bitter national struggle over the constitution was to uncover much
more about Malvern Chase, because local events were shaped by Charles I's
increasingly desperate measures to raise the money that he hoped would secure
his independence from a parliament critical of his policies. Charles was to be the
most obvious loser in these events, but his methods left us with some important
evidence about the forest and chase of Malvern.

X

Disafforestation

The disafforestation of Malvern Chase in the 17th century, a direct result of the financial straits of Charles I, is an excellent example of interaction between local and national history, reinforcing the importance of seeing local history in the national context.

Within a very short time of succeeding to the throne Charles I was in conflict with parliament. By 1629 he had, somewhat short-sightedly, resolved not to call parliament unless it was unavoidable – a course of action which threw him back on sources of revenue requiring no parliamentary approval. Some of his methods of raising money – the collection of ship-money, for example – became notorious, not least for the publicity attracted by challenges to them. One source which has attracted less attention is his giving up forest rights in return for money.

Worcestershire by this time contained two forests – Malvern and Feckenham. The latter was the first to be dealt with in 1629, the king imagining that he could disguise his hopes for personal gain as a measure to please the forest inhabitants:

> For the improving of his highness's revenue … and for the benefit and ease of his loving subjects, his majesty was resolved to disafforest, improve, and convert to his highness's best profit, amongst other forests his majesty's forest of Feckenham.[*]

As with many of Charles I's ideas, his *loving subjects* were not easily won over to his point of view. Rioting showed the unpopularity of his plans for Feckenham Forest but did not deter the king from doing the same thing in Malvern Forest. He had Malvern Chase mapped, surveyed and valued in 1628. The surviving map[†] is the earliest detailed map of this area and, with the survey,[‡] gives quite detailed evidence of the landscape at that time. The surveyors, Elias Allen and Richard Danes, listed the owners of land and valued the areas they owned. From this we can deduce the parishes then considered to comprise the forest but, as we have seen, there is, and apparently always was, great difficulty in defining its boundaries. The parishes named in 1628 were Berrow, Birtsmorton, Castlemorton, Hanley Castle, Great Malvern, Little Malvern, Longdon, Upton, Welland, the Link (part of Leigh), Mathon, Colwall and Bromsberrow. The 1628 survey also included Ledbury, which was part of the Bishop of Hereford's chase,

---

[*] T.R.Nash, *Collections for the History of Worcestershire,*1799 Vol.I, p.lxvii.
[†] Deposited with the Society of Antiquaries, which has kindly given permission for reproduction in this book.
[‡] Transcribed by E.A.B. Barnard and published in the 1929 *Transactions of the Worcestershire Archaeological Society,* pp.137-41.

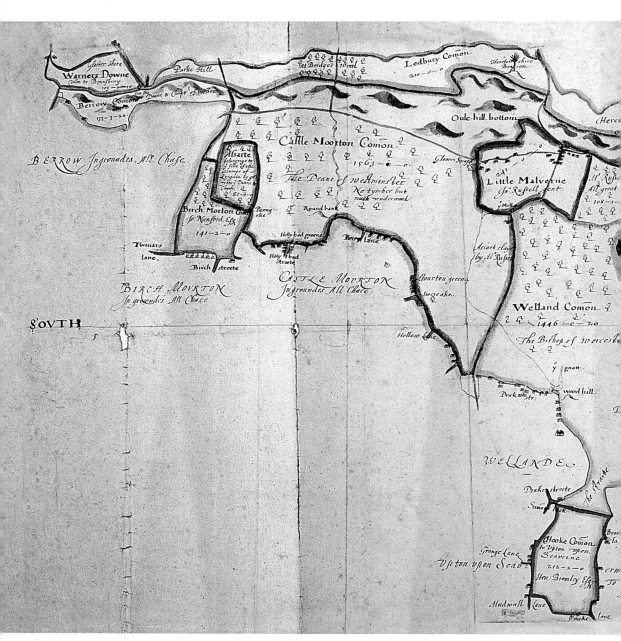

39 *The 1628 survey of Malvern Chase is the oldest surviving map to indicate the extent and boundaries of Malvern Chase. Note that the orientation puts north on the right-hand side. Clearly marked are most of the 13 parishes valued for Charles I so that he could establish how much money he might raise from the sale of a third of the wastelands on which intercommoning was practised. Parishes marked are Hanley, Little Malvern, Great Malvern ('Much Malverne'), Welland, Castlemorton, Upton, Colwall ('Collaway'), Mathon ('Matherne'), Birtsmorton ('Birch Morton') and Berrow. Although Leigh is not specifically marked, 'The Lynke' was then part of it. Bromsberrow and Longdon, towards the southern end of the Chase and adjacent to the*

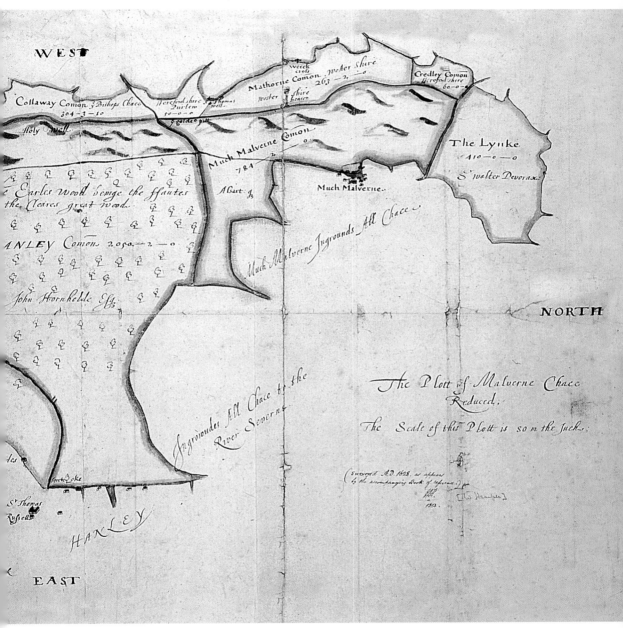

Gloucestershire forest areas, are not marked. Assarts, for which the king or lord of the chase had granted licence to clear, may be clearly seen in four distinct areas: between Birtsmorton and Castlemorton, in Little Malvern ('Mr Russell's Sarte. All great trees'), the western end of Welland ('claymed by Mr Russell'), and Great Malvern. Other landmarks are the Holy Well and two trees which were clearly of some significance, both called 'swete oke', in Castlemorton and in Hanley. Both the Herefordshire and the Worcestershire beacon sites are depicted with rough sketches. The area now known as Danemore Cross is shown as 'Dank Moor' suggesting a boggy area.

and Cradley Common. Although Nash explicitly states that it was not part of Malvern Chase, Cradley is shown on both the 1628 and 1633 maps as part of the chase lying in Herefordshire.

The 'Perticuler Survaie of the Kings Majesty's Chace of Malverne in the Countyes of Worcester, Hereford and Gloucester,' put the total acreage at just over 8,092 acres. There were 7,362 acres and 3 roods in Worcestershire, 626 acres 3 roods and 20 perches in Herefordshire and 103 acres and 20 perches in Gloucestershire. In fact there are discrepancies within the document and the total is probably nearer 8,135 acres. For example, the richest landholder in the chase, John Hornyold, was said to hold 2,050 acres but the details show this as

> above seaventeene hundred and ninety Acres worth xiij^s iiij^d the Acre, and of the hills neere three hundred wch soile is not worth above ij^s vj^d on the lower part being the fflatts and the cleeres there is great trees but little Tymber, and much other good underwood to whome the same belongeth ... but the fforesters say it belongeth to the Tennants and Lord of hanley others saie to the kinge.

So Hornyold's land totalled nearer 2,090 acres and was worth just over £1,230 in rents per year. Disputed ownership is also evident – as one might have expected.

Also, as one might expect, the church owned extensive areas, three leading churchmen having rights with a total value of about £1,294 and involving nearly half the land. The Dean of Worcester had nearly 400 acres in Mathon and Berrow, but it was 'all hillye and the soile course' with a total value of only about £50. The Bishop of Worcester did rather better with 1,446 acres of good land in Welland, worth about £723:

> The Bushops wood or Welland Common which adioyeth North to the deanes wood, and lyeth North on Hanlyes wast, which part of the wast is all on the fflatt, much plaine noe tymber but good underwood and the Land is well worth 10 shillings the Acre.

He also had

> One other parcell of Wast called the Bushops Acre adioyning North and lying North on the Earles wood or Hanly common noe Tymber but Braky Land, the Soyle worth x shillings the acre.

The Dean of Westminster had just over 1,563 acres in Castlemorton worth about £521. References to his lands include the following:

> Beginning at Ledburie waie and extending North as the Shire ditch runneth on the height of the hills to Herefordshire Beacon and thence to old yate head, where Hanley wood meetes, and thence descending East to Mr Russells Assart. ... There is within the said Waste one assart of fower score Acres belonging to the Lord thereof but graunted by Lease unto John Renford with the scite of the Mannor of Longdon. In which wast there is not anie Tymber but great stoare of good underwood. The Soyle is worthe by the Acre vj^s viij^d

John Russell, with his 241 acres around Little Malvern, held the best land, worth 16 shillings an acre. He also 'claymed ... wast ... full of verry good trees'. These 118 acres of wasteland were valued at 10 shillings an acre so his total holding was worth over £251.

Henry Bromley, lord of the manor of Upton, had 212 acres

> called the hoock. ...It was all great woods, but now all verry plain. The Soyle is well worth x^s the acre and better.

He also had much of the land around Malvern itself:

> One other parte of the said Chace called the Assart or much Malverne Comon belonging under the hill and conteyneth ccxxvij Acres iij roodes wheron there is good underwood, and the soile worth 10s the Acre. There is above the Town uppon the hills one other parte of the wast likewise belonging to Much malverne which conteyneth v^{c}lvj acres 3 roodes, which wast is all plaine, and not worth above ij^s vj^d the Acre.

Land to the north of Malvern, 410 acres for which no valuation was given, was held by Sir Walter Devereux:

> One other part of the said Chace called the Lyncke all plaine but some Brakes in some part and belongeth to the Lords Mannor.

Land in Birtsmorton was held by John Nanfan:

> The soil thereof is a third sorte, where in there is noe Tymber but some course Bracks on Bushes, by the Acre vj^s viij^d

Much of the Worcestershire acreage was 'hillie and plain ... and not worth above ij^s vi ^{d} the acre' while most of the Herefordshire area was worth even less – two shillings an acre. Quality of land was determined by several factors. The nature of the soil was obviously important, as was the amount and quality of the timber on it. Hillside land was clearly less valuable than the flat wasteland in Welland, while the worst land was described as 'plaine and barren'. Analysis of the survey points to 7,276 acres being worth approximately £3138 and no valuation being given for the remaining 859 acres.

The king wanted more details in order not only to ascertain the commercial value of the forest lands but also to try to find ways in which locals might be encouraged to be co-operative in his money-raising plans. Whilst hunting rights were of no particular interest to him, he hoped to be able to make use of his right to them by giving them up in exchange for one third of the wasteland, or common land, within the forest. Such newly acquired land had but one attraction – he could sell it for what he really needed – cash. As in all his policies, he was hopeful of getting his own way. He seemed to think that locals might welcome such a deal which would free them from the constraints of forest law. His calculations overlooked the fact that forest law had been implemented so haphazardly for so long that locals ignored it – apparently with impunity.

Sensibly, however, he found out which men were especially rich and influential, knowing that it would be worth treating them with particular care. If they accepted disafforestation, lesser men would follow. He appointed commissioners who were given careful and precise instructions in 'Articles of instruction to be inquired ... and executed by his Majesties commissioners authorised touchinge the disafforestacon and improveing of the fforeste or Chace of Malverne'.* Its first paragraph refers to Malvern Chase as containing two parts: the King's Chase in

---

* WRO 714 228.102/1.

the counties of Worcestershire and Gloucestershire and the Bishop's Chase in the county of Herefordshire.

The first task facing the commissioners raised the old problem of defining the boundaries of the chase. They were to

> repayre to the sayd fforest or chase or to some convenient place neere adjoining and as well by the ... depositions of witnesses as by your owne view ... to inquire and finde out the circuit and boundary of the said fforest or chase ... accordinge as the same hath bene and is nowe in use and reputed or known by the names of the King's Chase and the Bishopp's Chase and of the waste and comonable lande within the same.

Here is further evidence that nowhere was there set down – and probably never had been – any precise boundary to the forest.

The commissioners' second task gives further evidence of both the general level of ignorance and the laxity of forest authorities in enforcing forest law. It also shows the king's strong interest in the financial goings-on, indicating his determination to use forest rights as a potential source of money. The commissioners were to ascertain what new buildings had been erected on the wasteland during the last 40 years, by what warrants they had been built, and

> whoe are the pretended owners of the same ... whose possession the same now are and who receive the profitt thereof.

Thirdly, making a distinction between such newly enclosed land and land which had long been in private occupation, they were to find out what buildings had been put up during the last 40 years on privately occupied land which had long been enclosed. They were also to ascertain whether any 'anncient houses and tenements have bene devided into severall dwellings' and if so by what authority and to whose benefit.

The fourth task was a refinement of the second. Together they highlight the fact that, whatever the law decreed, there had been erosion of the waste or common land through its being taken into exclusive private ownership, apparently without challenge. The king's men were to see 'what land or ground have bene inclosed and assarted out of the waste' in the last 40 years, together with information on any buildings put on it. This would include on whose authority such buildings were erected, 'whoe are nowe the pretended owners or present possessors or occupiers ... and to whome the yearly rent or profitt thereof doth accrue'.

The fifth task of the commissioners is perhaps the most telling indictment of central government for its total ignorance of forest law and custom. It very effectively reinforces the argument that the implementation of forest law was haphazard. They had to

> informe yourselves what store of Deere are now kepte within the sayd fforest or chase or in other adjacent places which are known to be his Majesties game of Deere ... and what Officers are necessarilie attendant in the same in respecte of the sayd game of deere what fees or yeerely allowance they receive from his Majesty and what els is by them yeerely taken or made by virtue or coloure of their sayd places and what number of Deere are yeerely killed within the same fforest or chase, by whome and by what warrant and what the profitt doe yeerely accreue to his Majesty eyther by soyle sale of wood or timber or otherwise other then the feede of his Majesty's game of deere only.

example, the gentlemen benchers or who benefited from the fines. After Baxter mentioned the benchers so did Tipping and Simmonds. Similarly, after Mann mentioned the beneficiaries of the fines so did Bray and Edge.

The record of the proceedings gives ample evidence not only of the total ignorance of officialdom as to the laws theoretically applied to the chase but also a naivety in their methods of seeking to ascertain them. From the witness replies, it is clear that the officials sought and recorded any crumb of information, their original questions seeking the most basic facts. The results of each section in the inquiry may be summarised as follows:

1. *What is your name, age and place of residence? How long have you known Malvern Chase?*
   This ascertained the credentials of the witnesses who were clearly hand-picked for their extensive experience and knowledge. The youngest was Henry Dingley who had recorded his perambulation of the chase and was now 40 years old, while the oldest, aged 93, had known the chase for 60 years. The record period of familiarity with the chase was the 70 years claimed by 79 year old William Knight of Great Malvern. Some had official positions in the chase or connections with an officer. Dingley was a rider, Browne was a keeper and Edge had 'heard his father report, being a very old and ancient keeper'.

2. *What do you believe to be the boundaries of the chase?*
   This was to ascertain the extent of the chase but answers may not have been complete. John Browne listed 13 constituent parishes with which another three witnesses agreed. But other places were mentioned by some deponents whilst others may also have been in the chase but not mentioned by the witnesses, some of whom were quite vague in their answers.

3. *What is the status of Hanley Castle? What rights do its inhabitants have in the chase?*
   Answers relating to Hanley Castle and its inhabitants indicate wide agreement that it was a special part of Malvern Chase and that its inhabitants could pick up windfall wood (common of estovers) but could be fined by chase officials if they actually felled wood and carried it off.

4. *Do the Cliffey and Link woods have keepers? Can Hanley Castle residents cut down wood in them?*
   There was wide agreement about the appointment by the chief forester of keepers for the Cliffey and Link woods. Richard Edge, who had known the chase for 30 years said that his father, as a keeper in the Cliffey wood, had taken attachments there. Richard Tipping and several others confirmed that keepers could take attachments. Thomas Mann and John Burford offered the further detail that two-thirds of such fines went to the queen and one third to the chief forester. This makes it clear that it was in the interests of the chief forester to appoint men who would perform their duties vigilantly and enable prosecutions to be made. Two of the witnesses referred to the benchers who sat at or near Hanley Church, 'for reformation of disorders of the chase'. Both witnesses claimed to know little about the benchers, who seem no longer to have been in existence by 1589. Indeed several of the customs of the chase seem by then to have been but distant memories.

5. *What happens if deer go into the manor of Hanley Castle?*
It was generally agreed that deer were free to wander and graze wherever they wished in the chase, including in Hanley, except for that part of Hanley known as Blackmore 'which is a park enclosed'. As was the case in other parts of the chase, residents were not allowed to drive off the deer – which prohibition pinpoints the greatest problem faced by chase inhabitants struggling to farm. It was, however, legal for the keepers to enter 'without any let or trespass' upon any part of Hanley to drive out deer.

A careless attitude to forest administration clearly prevailed in the later Middle Ages and the early 16th century. This led to certain benefits for modern enquirers because it created a situation which encouraged late 16th-century officials to pose exactly the sort of questions which later historians would wish to have answered.

Within 50 years much more information was to emerge, as 17th-century parliaments challenged the Stuart kings who proclaimed belief in their divine right to rule. The bitter national struggle over the constitution was to uncover much more about Malvern Chase, because local events were shaped by Charles I's increasingly desperate measures to raise the money that he hoped would secure his independence from a parliament critical of his policies. Charles was to be the most obvious loser in these events, but his methods left us with some important evidence about the forest and chase of Malvern.

Other animals were dealt with in their sixth task – to find out how many sheep, goats and cattle were kept on the wasteland in the forest, and to whom they belonged. Given the scorn of the countryman for the foolish and the self-important, locals must have relished the fun of giving answers to such questions emanating from London.

One wonders, too, what the locals would have made of attempts to discover

> what losse or damadge doeth yeerely accrewe to any the inhabitants and comoners ... by reason of the game of deere and foreste lawe-suit in Starr Chamber for Killinge of deere or otherwise in doeinge or committinge any thinge contrary to the fforest lawes and liberties ... and in what manner in what measure and by what meanes they have susteyned such losse or damadge.

The elementary nature of the facts sought in the eighth task gives yet more proof that for years no interest whatever had been taken in the forest. The commissioners were to find out what wood or soil the king owned in the forest,

> where the same lieth and by what name or names the same are reputed and known ... what wood or timber hath bene sold or otherwise disposed of by any the Officers ... or any other person ... and howe the profitt thereof hath bene answered to his late Majesty or his nowe Majesty and what other timber trees or wood have bene felled and disposed of [in the last forty years].

The ninth task, like the sixth, struck at the heart of common grazing rights. The commissioners were to find out what cattle commoners grazed, where they grazed them ... 'and by what right they soe challendge or enjoy the same comon'.

The tenth order – which one may be tempted to think might have come higher in the list – was to win over the locals. This was a daunting task, in view of the sudden arrival of officials poking their noses into local affairs after a long period of obvious laxity. They were to

> warne and call before you all or as many owners tenants Occupiers Inhabitants Comoners Officers and other persons interested within the said fforeste or Chase as to you shall seeme meete and propounde and offer unto them in his Majesty's behalfe the disafforestation of the sayd fforeste or Chase and to treate with all such persons as have intereste of Comon or other lawfull righte or clayme ... and ... to allowe them ... such quantities of the said waste ... answerable in value for their sayd interest ... and assigned out of that parte of waste which is his Majesty's soyle ... to bee granted in ffee simple ffee ffarme or by lease as you shall agree ...

The king's desperation to reach agreement with the locals is very clear, urging

> that you use your best endeavours as well by further treaties with such person or persons whom it may any way concerne as by your wisdom and discrecons touching the porsons or allotments out of his Majesty's parte in severaltie freede from all comonage as much of the sayd fforeste as possibly you cann.

Desirous of securing an advantageous allocation of land to himself, the king naively supposed that locals could be persuaded that they were being offered a bargain in the shape of land and freedom from forest law with all its inconveniences. They must be told

> of the greate benefitt the subjecte shall receive for their parte ... in respecte ...
> disburtheninge of their other land and wood within the sayd fforeste ... both from
> the game of deere and from the chardges of fforest lawes as also of a full and free
> discharge of all offences comitted and done by them in manner aforesaid.

Possibly somewhat grudgingly, recognising that every property owner had a
duty to help with the maintenance of the poor, the commissioners were instructed
to consider how much waste needed to be allowed

> for reliefe of the poore sorte of Inhabitante ... and that ... you doe allott the same
> places convenient in such manner as may bee agreeable with his Majesties honour
> albeit by the lawes of this land they cannot justly challendge or claime to have
> any righte att all.

Finally they were told to do their best to get the king what he wanted:

> That you further informe yourselves by all ways and meanes you can of all other
> matters and things as in your wisedoms and discrecons you shall conceive requisite
> to bee considered of any way touchinge or concerninge the p'misses for the better
> and more speedy expeditinge and furtheringe his Majesty's pleasure and profitt
> herein

This document shows an attempt – if clumsy – to comply with accepted law
and custom and to win the support of those most closely affected. Some months
later, details were drawn up of a disafforestation decree, the effects of which
were immediate. The 1632 disafforestation decree explained changes to be made
in the forest or chase, which was 'as well known by the name of the Bishop's
Chase as by the name of the King's Chase'. These changes would have the effect
of depriving local inhabitants of the use of one-third of the wasteland on which,
since time immemorial, they had exercised common rights such as grazing and
the right to collect windfall wood. In return they would no longer have to suffer
the inconveniences of forest law.

> One third part of the waste or commonable lands ... should be set out, severed
> and divided, by indifferent commissioners and surveyors to be to that purpose
> appointed from the other two parts of the said waste ... and be held and enjoyed
> by his majesty, his heirs, successors, and assigns ... freed and discharged from the
> title of common therein. ... the other two parts of the said waste ... should remain
> and continue unto and amongst the commoners ... according to their several rights
> and interests, discharged from his majesty's game of deer there and of and from
> the forest laws.

The proposals produced the usual problem with new laws: hardly anybody
understood what was happening. Families who had for generations grazed their
animals in the chase and picked up windfall wood for heating their homes feared
– wrongly – that they would lose such rights. The whole area was in uproar,
local fears and anxieties doubtless fanned by rumours of how other men in
other counties had resisted this or that demand of the king and met with dire
punishment. The backdrop to all these local events was national disquiet about
the king's claim to rule by divine right.

Not unnaturally, the most influential landowners, led by descendants of the
robust landowners of the 16th century, challenged the disafforestation, which
would adversely affect their status. They had little to lose from challenging the

king and, as events were to prove, quite a lot to gain. Sir Thomas Russell (who had been the chief forest official) and John Hornyold (owner of the manor of Hanley which had been the seat of chase administration) were accused of inciting 'riots and other misdemeanours ... in opposition and hindrance of the execution of the said decree'. Unsurprisingly, the Lord Chief Justice, acting for the king, was unable to identify most of the rioters, while the supposed ring leaders naturally denied any part in the disturbances – countrymen were certainly not going to make life simple for urban authorities. Sir Thomas Russell and his son, Sir William Russell, played the card that the riots were due to difficulties in understanding what, exactly, was going on and urged the king to clarify the situation, suggesting that 'if those mistakings might be rectified, the county would be well satisfied'.

People needed the assurance that

> none of the lands of the said forest ... shall be taken in, or enclosed, but only his majesty's third part ... and that the other two third parts shall be left open and free for the freeholders and tenants and commoners to take their common of pasture and common of eastovers therein as heretofore they have been accustomed; with this express restriction ... that no ... lords of ... manors whatsoever shall be permitted to enclose any part of the two third parts of the said chase or to fall the woods or trees ... whereby the commoners may be hindered of their eastovers.

There was, of course, anxiety that the king might take the best land, and the 1630 document's instructions to his commissioners to get as advantageous a deal as possible suggests that this anxiety was well founded. There was, however, a written undertaking that the king's third was 'not to be purposely chosen, or picked out of the best'. It must be 'indifferently allotted ... good and bad proportionably'.

By great good fortune another 17th-century map has also been preserved: it is in the Berington archives deposited in Worcestershire Record Office.* Berington predecessors at Little Malvern were the Russells, who may well have commissioned the drawing of the map. Drawn at the time (probably 1633) that disafforestation was being carried out, it appears to be incomplete, since routes and boundaries which led to Upton-upon-Severn and other chase parishes stop abruptly at the map's bottom edge. Nevertheless, what has survived is a delightful as well as informative piece of written evidence, showing routes and places of note such as the beacons on top of the hills, and indicating how plots of land were laid out. These plots, of considerable acreage, show how the interests of various parishes and individuals were to be safeguarded.

It is no surprise that some of the bigger landowners, such as Hornyold and Russell, appear to have been bought off, a state of affairs foreseen by the instructions in 1630 to the commissioners to use their wisdom and discretion in dealing with challenges to the proposals. Their reward for withdrawing opposition to disafforestation came in the form of land grants – 'the same to be performed out of the third part allotted ... to his majesty ... and not out of the other two parts that are to remain to the country'. Hornyold also had guaranteed to him his traditional rent-oats and rent-hens from inhabitants of Colwall, Mathon and Great Malvern.

---

* WRO X 705:24 Mrs T.M. Berington and the County Archives Manager have kindly given permission for its reproduction in this book.

So it was all settled: local leaders got their cut and other locals were assured that no more wasteland would ever disappear into private hands. Furthermore, all the fencing necessary to separate the king's third from the other two-thirds was to be erected and maintained at the expense of the king or anyone who received from him any part of what came to be known as Thirds Land.

For the first time in nearly six centuries substantial areas of land could legally be developed, though a modern developer would be stopped in his tracks by the requirement that every new cottage must sit in a plot of at least 20 acres. Later development of the plot was apparently forbidden, since it had to be 'continued':

> that no new cottage shall be erected on any part of the said third part ... whereunto there shall not be layed and continued twenty acres at the least.

No new cottage could be built

> but such only as shall be warranted by the law and statutes made for the mainte-nance and provision of the poor.

New property owners were thus reminded that, in acquiring or improving prop-erty, they would be required to shoulder their share of the rate levied to help the poor. Anyone who came to own land in the king's third had to contribute

> to the charge of the church and poor in the several parishes where the same shall lie, and to all other public charges ... in a due and fit proportion.

Charles I's life and reign ended with his 1649 execution. Was disafforestation that elusive creature – a successful policy initiated by this controversial mon-arch? Hardly – as a revenue raiser it provided a drop in the ocean of funds he needed. He sold his interest in the chase to Sir Cornelius Vermuyden for £5,000. Vermuyden and his associate, the Attorney General Sir Robert Heath, planned to get back their money by leasing or selling off parcels of land – an enterprise which proved disappointing for them.[*]

From the early 1630s the area had seen much disturbance and it had proved difficult to enclose the areas allotted as the king's third. In November 1633, when the work of enclosure was still incomplete

> divers disorderly persons had entered into the remaining two third parts limited to the Lords, Tenants and Commoners and had there cut down and carried away the greatest part of the Timber Trees and many hundred young oaks and saplings insomuch that all the orderly and well disposed Tenants and Commoners which had right of Common of Estovers within the said two parts would not be able to dwell and inhabit in their ancient houses but in great distress. ... for several years [it was complained]amongst other things ... that the Commoners would not execute the necessary conveyances to perfect the title to the King's third. ... Meantime Sir Cornelius Vermuyden transferred his interest in the Chase to Sir William Russell and George Strode ... There does not appear to be any further record respecting the division of the Chase until the year 1658 when the Attorney General of the Commonwealth filed another information complaining that certain Inhabitants within the Chase had thrown down inclosures made in pursuance of the decree of [disafforestation].[†]

* Brian S. Smith, *A History of Malvern*, 1978, p.155.
† WRO 705:79.

Local inhabitants were bitter that they had not been properly consulted:

> they were not parties to the proceedings which had resulted in that decree and
> had been deprived of their common without compensation. ...The King, it is stated
> enjoyed his third for 8 or 9 years before the Civil War but since the beginning
> of War parts of the enclosures forming the Third had been broken down by the
> Commoners.

Eventually an injunction was taken out

> restraining the Commoners temporarily from disturbing the holders of the King's
> Third and the issuing of a Commission to treat with persons who had not yet
> submitted to the Disafforestation.

Disafforestation and its effects should be seen in a national context of anger
and eventually rebellion against a king trying to implement controversial policies
in all major areas of government, such as finance, religion and – the crux of
the matter – the role of the monarch in the constitution. A spirit of challenge
and lawlessness prevailed for much of the period 1630 to 1660, as the country
travelled the inexorable path from questioning the king's authority, through open
rebellion and ultimately to the first trial and execution of a monarch in Europe.
Various attempts at forming a satisfactory government without a king led in 1660
to a return to monarchy in the person of Charles II – an accomplished politician,
who had learned his skills in a hard school.

Did forest inhabitants come to accept the changes which they had so vigor-
ously opposed? In 1661 representatives from former chase parishes made formal
declarations as to what they perceived as the effects of disafforestation. Although
some grumbled that they had never assented to the changes, others had no doubt
about their benefits. In Welland, Robert Boulter, who had been a keeper in the
chase, remembered that before disafforestation

> The game of deere did very much dampnify* the owners of lands within the
> precincts of the said Chace by their eateing of the commoners' corne and other
> commodities ... Hee hath with his hounds hunted 40 deere ... at a tyme out of the
> owners corne and lands nere the said chace. †

His neighbour, John White of Welland, claimed that things were now much
better:

> The parishes of Hanley Castle, parte of Castlemorton and Welland by the remove-
> ing of the game of Deere and by the setting out of the 3rd parte of the said Chace
> are greately improved and are thereby in their corne and pastures made of double
> the vallue of what they were when the game of Deere were mainteyned within
> and about the Chace aforesaid.‡

In 1664 Charles II agreed to the disafforestation initiated by his 'late father
of glorious memory', when he signed the Act 'for confirmation of the enclosure
and improvement of Malvern Chase'. By this time much had changed since the
original 1632 decree. By the early 1660s much of the king's third had passed to
others such as Sir Nicholas Strode. John Birch had that part of the third lying

---

* injure.
† WRO 714 228.102/2.
‡ *ibid.*

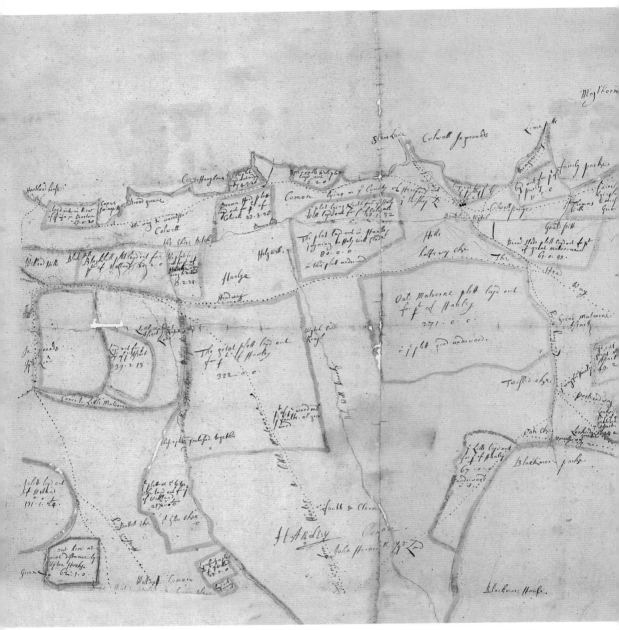

40   *The Berington map of Malvern Chase was drawn about five years later than the one drawn for Charles I, and provides further fascinating detail, though its extent does not stretch so far east or south. The most southerly land is marked as 'Welland Hills', just to the north of the Herefordshire Beacon, which is not shown. Major paths are marked, as are features such as 'Coxes swinepitt', 'Lime pitts' and the 'Gould pitt' which was the scene of some optimistic digging. The Worcestershire Beacon is quite artistically portrayed, and the Hornyold mansion of Blackmore House is singled out for mention, whilst the house later occupied by the Beringtons, Little Malvern Court, is not. It was, however, built on former monastic land*

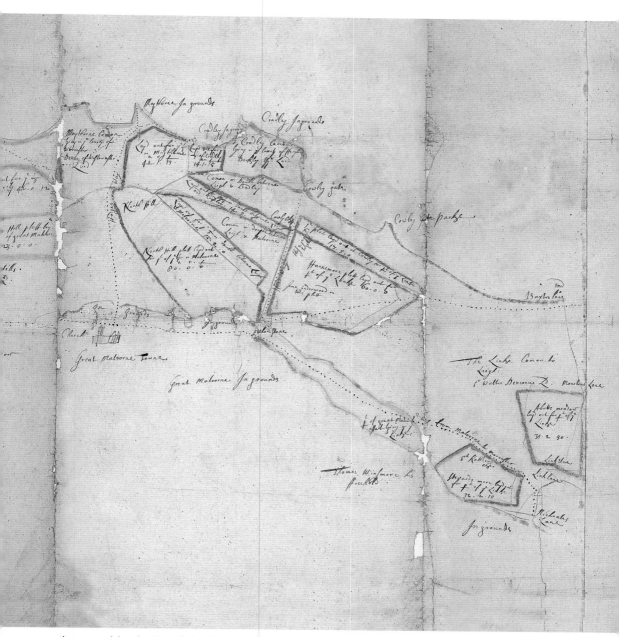

then owned by the Russell family. Little Malvern Priory Church, like Great Malvern Priory Church, is represented by a crudely drawn church – the only churches portrayed. On some plots a small ⅓ can be discerned – this indicates that it was part of the king's third of the wasteland. Some named trees ('twisted oke') present no particular mystery, but others give rise to a number of questions – was 'Battell oke', near Danemore crossroads, the site of a battle against the Danes? Or (see the earlier 1628 map) is Danemore, more prosaically, a corruption of 'dank'? Where was the traveller who reached 'halfeway oke' on the eastern slope of the hill coming from and going to?

in Herefordshire (leased from the bishop of Hereford) and William Thackwell had that part lying in Birtsmorton. The other two-thirds of the common land, supposedly left open and free forever, would be the focus of considerable dispute and legal action in years to come. Through all this turmoil the ordinary people, bewildered and impotent as ever, had no choice but to go along with the decisions of their social superiors who made the law and thus wielded an authority much more powerful than the farming implements of workers tearing down the fences erected around their former common land.

Those concerned at the loss of common rights were to be proved justified in their fears. For, notwithstanding the promises made in the decree, significant portions of the common land in fact fell into private hands through the twin perils of illegal encroachment and legal, if controversial, enclosure. Before examining the history of those broken promises, a consideration of the effects of the Civil War in this rural area may help to explain the anxieties of a population which nationally totalled 5½ million in the last half of the 17th century. Of these, about 80 per cent were directly or indirectly connected with agriculture and the land.[*]

---

* R.C. Gaut, *A History of Worcestershire Agriculture*, 1939, p.94.

XI

Malvern Chase during the Civil War

Worcestershire played a key role in the civil war between the Stuarts and Parliament – indeed, the final engagement between the son of the executed king and his opponents took place on 3 September 1651 at Worcester. It was a bloodbath. The longest period of fighting was between 1642 and 1646, with an uneasy peace until that final battle. Two hundred years later, when Worcester's Foregate Street railway bridge was built, it incorporated the legend *civitas in bello in pace fidelis*, perpetuating the notion that Worcester was faithful in war and peace to the Stuart cause. Malcolm Atkin[*] argues convincingly that this reputation is a myth not borne out by the facts. This is not the place for a detailed discussion of loyalties or for an account of the numerous military campaigns waged in the region at places such as Powick, Upton and Ledbury as well as Worcester itself. It is, however, worth noticing the effects – some of them long-lasting – of those campaigns here in an area still adapting to changes brought about by disafforestation.

All wars are paid for in terms of cash and life by ordinary people, and the chase parishes certainly paid their share. There are references to the early days of the war when, for example, Welland and Little Malvern jointly raised £3 11s. 0d. 'for the setting forth of a soldier'.[†] These expenses made no mention of weaponry, but included 13s. 4d. for four yards of cloth, one shilling 'for buttons and silke', 22d. 'for callico to line the skirt' and various small sums for 'pockets, hookes and eyes'. The soldier was provided with two shirts, one pair of shoes, a pair of stockings, a cap and a knapsack. 'Makinge of the apparell' cost a modest four shillings, compared with the expenses of Peter Tiler, the Constable of Little Malvern, who seems to have spent 6d 'when I tooke him' and a further three or four shillings 'for charges from Munday morninge untill Wednesday morninge and one to looke to him'. Then there was another three shillings 'for charges in Worcester for our dinners and other expenses for drinke'. Welland paid similar expenses, on top of their £2 share of the expenses for equipping the soldier. Enough survives of a damaged document[‡] for us to learn that in August 1642 the king was trying to get an army together. The constables of Welland, Little Malvern, Holdfast, Berrow and Pendock were instructed by the High Constable to summon

---

[*] Malcolm Atkin, *The Civil War in Worcestershire*, 1995, pp.151-2.
[†] W.R.O. 705:24/630.
[‡] W.R.O. 705:24/873.

all trained, freehold and clergy bands … both horse and foote … to appeare before the Commissioners upon the xijth day of this instant August being ye fryday in the morninge by ixen of the clock in the great meadowe called Pritchecrofte … compleatly armed and arrayed.

As so often in war, in their innocence of what was to come these officials and the young men sent to fight were probably intrigued by the unusual excitement of such a gathering, but bitter experiences were later to be endured. The fighting took a heavy toll, with Worcester itself in 1651 so full of dead bodies of men and horses that 'there was such nastiness a man could hardly abide in the town'.[*] The comment is scarcely surprising when one considers the magnitude of the task of disposing of the bodies of the 3,000, or perhaps even 4,000, men estimated[†] to have been killed between 2 p.m. and nightfall on 3 September 1651. J.W. Willis Bund, who in the 19th century immersed himself in the records of the Court of Quarter Sessions, had a telling reference to the wounded, too:

> The wounded soldiers were beyond count. Possibly the number will be best appreciated from the fact that for years after the Restoration whenever application was made by a pauper for relief to the Court of Quarter Sessions he invariably stated, almost as a common form, that he had been wounded at Worcester.[‡]

Willis Bund also claims that registers of parishes in the county reveal that 'many a wounded soldier … after the fight had wandered there to die'. If this is so, chase parishes will probably have been involved. In the 1640s and 1650s the keeping of parish registers was neglected but Upton-upon-Severn's register for 1644 records the burials of 'Jhon Hasell, slaine by a souldier' and of 'William Turberville, a souldier'.

Early in the war, in 1642, an encounter at Powick saw the dashing Prince Rupert and his troops rout the Parliamentarians, causing them to flee along the road to Upton, to cross the Severn there, en route for Pershore. Accounts vary as to the details of the clash, which took only minutes and was little more than

---

* J.W. Willis Bund, *The Civil War in Worcestershire*, p.253.
† J.W. Willis Bund, *The Civil War in Worcestershire*, p.251.
‡ J.W. Willis Bund, *op.cit.*, p.248.

41 *The old bridge at Powick.*

a skirmish, but it established Prince Rupert's reputation as a courageous and effective soldier and leader, despite his youth. He was only 22, but the events at Powick 'rendered the name of Prince Rupert very terrible and exceedingly appalled the adversary'.[*]

In December 1645 there was a skirmish at Malvern, when Parliamentarians crossed into Malvern from Herefordshire and met about 50 rather surprised royalist soldiers, of whom 28 were taken prisoner. The victors also took 50 horses.[†]

Upton-upon-Severn's medieval wooden bridge had been replaced in 1605 by a more substantial handsome structure with five arches in red sandstone. The only bridge across the Severn between Gloucester and Worcester, it quite often featured in the fighting, Parliamentarians and Royalists each holding it at different times. In 1643 Royalists took it from Parliamentarians who regained control of it in 1644. By

42 *Damage caused to the tower of Powick Church as Parliamentary soldiers advanced on Worcester in 1651.*

far the most dramatic exchange was to happen within days of the end of the war in 1651. By this time one arch of the bridge had been deliberately demolished to try to stop Parliamentary troops taking the town from Scottish soldiers supporting Charles I's son, Charles, who had taken up the cause of his executed father. Barely a mile up the road the Parliamentarian Nicholas Lechmere had to accept troops billeted at his home, Severn End, in Hanley Castle:

> Massie, Major-General to ye … King with about 130 Scottish horse quarter'd in my house at Hanley, hee treated my people civilly, but threatned extirpation to mee and my posterity bycause I was ioyn'd to the army of ye p'liamt.[‡]

Five days before the final battle of Worcester, Cromwell's Major-General Lambert sent 18 of his bravest men to negotiate a narrow plank across the damaged bridge over the Severn at risk of being fired upon by royalist supporters. As dawn broke on the morning of 29 August

> in dim daylight … high above a deep, rapid river … they did not shrink … When they got on to the plank, and began to march in single file, they could not stand the running water below them; their heads swam and they were in danger of falling. So they sat down on the plank, straddling across it, scrambling along. They mounted it as though it was their wooden Pegasus, and so scrambled across to the opposite side.[§]

---

[*] J.W.Willis Bund, *op.cit.* (quoting Clarendon), p.6.
[†] J.W. Willis Bund, *op.cit.*, pp.173-4.
[‡] E.P. Shirley, *Hanley and the House of Lechmere*, 1883.
[§] J.W.Willis Bund, *The Civil War in Worcestershire*, p.231.

Having reached the riverside churchyard, they locked themselves into the church and fired on the enemy who set fire to the church before being routed by reinforcements ordered by Lambert to wade through the river to help whoever still survived of his 18 stricken heroes in the church. Once in control of Upton, the Parliamentarians encamped no fewer than 12,000 troops on the west bank of the Severn. Cromwell himself came to thank Lambert's courageous men, and the scene was set for Parliament's ultimate victory at Worcester.

43 *Charles Cattermole's romantic 19th-century view of the battle for Upton Bridge, taken from Emily Lawson's* Records and Traditions of Upton-upon-Severn.

44 *Nash's 18th-century view of Severn End shows its closeness to the River Severn, on which the traditional barge, or trow, is portrayed.*

45 *Dr Nash's*
Worcestershire *contains this*
portrait of Judge Nicholas
Lechmere, who lived from 1613
until 1701 and recorded some
of the civil war turmoil.

Nicholas Lechmere at Severn End in Hanley Castle, like many others, saw merits and faults in both kings and parliaments. Personal loss or gain also had a bearing on the decision, and some surprising changes of loyalty occurred. Indeed, the Royalist Massey who had billeted troops with the indignant Lechmere was himself a former Parliamentarian commander who decided to join the royalist cause. Although Lechmere supported Parliament during the war, in 1660 he paid to 'the most excellent Prince Charles ye second King of England' £200 for a royal pardon, enabling him to continue to build up his family estates. For Upton the long-term effects of the war were rather less happy, its damaged bridge and church both becoming a long-standing drain on its resources.

Worcestershire suffered more than most counties from the plundering of both Royalists and Parliamentarians. Since Worcestershire was in the thick of so much of the fighting, its churches suffered, puritan supporters of parliament having little respect for what they saw as idolatrous imagery in churches. Churchwardens' presentments prove that numerous chase churches were in a very bad state of repair in the years after the civil war. The causes are not always clear, as in Welland in 1663 when 'our church is downe and churchyard is in good repaire'. By 1674 'our parish church body and chancell is newly built and finished, the steeple wants repairing'.

There is, however, definite documentary evidence of extensive war damage to some churches, such as Upton and Castlemorton, where in 1662

> The Church, Chappell and Chansell by reason of ye late tymes and the late great wildness [?] was very much out of order within and without, but much hath beene don this sumer towarde the repayers thereof, the perfecting the repayers thereof are indevouring to be doe in althings according to ye Artickles with all convenient speede.

46 & 47 *Maria Martin's early 19th-century sketches of Welland church which had been rebuilt after the civil war. This church was replaced by a neo-Gothic church on a new site in the centre of the parish in 1875.*

By 1674 some windows in Castlemorton Church had been broken in a storm but the building was 'lately new seated and pewed'. John Noake in the 1850s was told the story behind this new seating by the old parish clerk, whom he suspected of adding 'not a few embellishments of his own'. Certainly the date, 1682, given by this oral tradition for the new pews is eight years later than the 1674 churchwardens' presentment, but the claims that in the 1640s parliamentarians had made a bonfire of the seats of Castlemorton Church seem authentic. It appears that a group of royalists had retreated to the tower and

> as a body of the rebels came up the lane ... peppered them right royally ... But the ungodly faction were not thus to be driven away; and having forced themselves into the church, they tore up the seats, and made such a bonfire that being fairly roasted on the tower, [the royalists] were fain to take off their coats and breeches to stand upon, ... but they were soon smothered and fell, like Lucifer, ne'er to rise again.[*]

One of the surprises to be found in churchwardens' presentments and other documentation is the speed with which bad conditions could be put right by quite small populations. For example, despite all the damage to Castlemorton

---

* John Noake, *The Rambler in Worcestershire*, 1854, p.22.

Church, by 1674 the bishop's representative visiting Castlemorton found it 'in good order, with the utensills, vestments, bookes and ornaments of same; there is wanting onely a decent communion table'.* The neighbouring small parish of Welland had totally rebuilt its church in the same period, as we have seen.

At Little Malvern, too, where the undersides of the carved misericord seats were hacked off, war damage was serious. In 1662,

> As concerning our church it is out of repair at present in regard of the late warrs which did so impoverish the people that they were not able to repair it, it being known to be a very small and poore place, but we hope in some time to have it put in order with other things necessary.

It was indeed a very small and poor parish, able to offer only a miserable stipend of £5 a year to its minister, necessarily non-resident since there was not even a parsonage house or any glebe land.

> Concerning the minister he doth read divine service and preach to us and is a man of good life and conversation which he did at our request the meanes being so small that there was no man ever instituted and inducted to it.

After the defeat of Charles I and his execution in 1649 congregations were also confused by, and often resentful of, changes imposed by parliament on religious life. For example, Upton's parson, William Woodford, was replaced, like

---

* Paul Morgan (ed.), *Inspections of churches and parsonage houses in the Diocese of Worcester*, 1986, p.24.

48   *Castlemorton Church in the early 20th century.*

49 & 50   *The surviving east end of Little Malvern Priory Church was seriously damaged during the civil war fighting. These 19th-century prints show the picturesque exterior and the rather bleak interior.*

so many clergymen at that time, by a minister more to the taste of parliament. He never moved far away and was re-instated when the monarchy was restored in 1660, dying in 1662. The poor old man – he had been inducted to Upton in 1624 – must have been saddened to see not only the damage to so many local churches, including his own, but also the mess made in his carefully kept register book during his enforced absence. The horrors of the years of fighting are not clear from the registers in which few entries were made. The two victims of fighting recorded as being buried in Upton in 1644 cannot have been the only victims in Upton of the war. So few burials attributed to war can scarcely reflect the realities of bloodshed and crimes resulting from it.

Soldiers were irregularly paid and caused great distress in the areas through which they passed, rampaging about the countryside like armed robbers. When, in 1644, Prince Rupert was created Duke of Cumberland by a grateful Charles I, the parliamentarians were quick to adapt his title to 'Prince Robber, Duke of Plunderland'.* They were not, however, speaking from particularly high moral ground, being themselves as guilty of plundering as their opponents. Sometimes the damage and intrusion into the lives of individuals were on a large scale, despite the efforts of the so-called Clubmen, who were groups of countrymen established to try to stop plundering by both sides

> If you offer to plunder, or take our cattle,
> Rest assured we will give you battle.†

Some property owners, such as John Hornyold of Blackmore Park, paid protection money to both sides to try to avoid being plundered. In Hornyold's case it was the large sum of £12 a month to each side.‡ But then, failure to buy off the plunderers came dear, too, and private individuals sometimes suffered significant loss. In Castlemorton, Nash records that in September 1643

> One hundred and fifty three soldiers, some from Gloucester, and some from Tewkesbury, taking advantage of the neighbourhood being absent at Ledbury fair … came to Castlemorton to plunder Mr Rowland Bartlett's house; a man so well beloved in his country, for his hospitality – so dear to all sorts of people, especially to the poor, for his charity, and those helps which he freely bestowed upon them – that had not the rebels taken the opportunity of his neighbours being at the fair, the force had been too weak to have plundered his house. In Mr Bartlett's chamber Scriven seized Mrs Bartlett's watch, and breaking open a chest took away £600, besides linen to the value of £60; and in other rooms they found more money, plate, jewels, bracelets, etc. … In their strict search they met with Mrs Bartlett's sweetmeats: these they scattered on the ground, not daring to taste of them for fear of poison. After this poor Mr Bartlett's house was plundered four or five times.§

Mr Bartlett's experiences do add a little substance to a claim made in October 1643 at the manorial court in Upton. There had been frequent excuses for the authorities' failure to provide a ducking-stool for the punishment of dishonest tradesmen as well as nagging wives. The offender was strapped into the seat, sometimes called a *goomstool,* and dipped into a pond – in Upton's case a stagnant

---

* J.W. Willis Bund, *The Civil War in Worcestershire*, p.115.
† J.W. Willis Bund, *op.cit.*, p.149.
‡ J.W. Willis Bund, *op.cit.*, p.152.
§ T.R. Nash, *Collections for the History of Worcestershire*, Vol. II, 1799, p.110 and John Noake, *The Rambler in Worcestershire*, 1854, p.25.

pool often used for the disposal of garbage. In 1643 Upton people found their best excuse ever for their lack of a ducking-stool:

> Wee present wee have noe goomstoole but we doe desire a time to make it by the reason of the troublesome times wee did not provide to get it for feare that it would bee broken downe by the souldiers.*

In Welland a poor widow petitioned the Bishop of Worcester in the 1660s because soldiers had stolen not only her belongings but also the deeds to her property:

> May it please your lordship, these are to certifie that Ann Pewtres of Welland in your Countie hath beene plundered by soldiers both of her goods, chattles and of severall writtings which did verie nearely conserne her estate not only deeds muniments and other but alsoe of her coppie of Court Roll by which she holds ... pasture ground ...
>   In ye late troubles there were some that showed and confessed they had them in possession and would returne backe her said writings if in consideration thereof she would presently deposite unto them the some of tenn pounds which by reason of her verie great losses and sufferings she was made altogeather unable to pay being so considerable a some and she soe impoverished by ye late plunder and ... thereupon they departed carringe her said writings with them. And that she hath since made inquirie after them but they being straingers could never heare of them nor in whose hands those writings now are.†

Richer pickings were taken by the authorities from wealthy landowners such as the Hornyolds of Hanley Castle. General Monck, parliamentarian soldier who eventually facilitated the restoration of the monarchy, told the king that John Hornyold was the greatest sufferer from the rebellion in Worcestershire. His son, Thomas Hornyold, was taken prisoner after the battle of Worcester, from which he helped the future Charles II to escape. In 1661 Thomas appealed to Charles II:

> That your petitioner hath served your Majestie and your late Royall ffather of ever blessed memory in all the warres to the ruine of himselfe and family by plunder sequestration and cuttinge downe of woods to the value of five thousand pounds and upwards.
> That he attended your majesty at your coming to Worcester with a troop of horse raised at his owne charge and was therefore found guilty by a grand jury at an Assize at Worcester of treason against the State ‡

The chase landscape must have been dramatically changed by such extensive destruction of woodland. Nor did the family have all its estates returned to it when the monarchy was restored.§

It is stating the obvious to say that the 17th century was a troubled period in our national history as attempts to address constitutional and religious issues tore the country apart. Rather less obviously, for those who lived in former chase parishes such national issues were complicated by local ones, as the effects of disafforestation became more apparent. Succeeding generations of lawyers were to find this fertile ground for business.

---

*   WRO 899: 93/2.
†   WRO 009.1 BA 2636/150.
‡   WRO BA1751 705:295/5.
§   *Victoria County History*, Vol.IV, p.96.

XII

Broken Promises and Developments in the Eighteenth and Nineteenth Centuries

After so many centuries of forest law locals were free from the limitations it had imposed on their use of land. The consequences were not obvious or dramatic, though the land acquired by the king, having passed through the hands of Vermuyden and Heath, offered opportunities to set up new farms and extend other estates. In former chase parishes numerous houses date from the 17th century.

The remaining two-thirds of wasteland continued to be used much as before. Indeed, for generations the area was still referred to as Malvern Chase. In 1726 a freehold estate in Hanley Castle, was advertised with 'a good new-built house', and described as 'situate within 100 yards of Malvern Chace',[*] and a Castlemorton vestry meeting minute of January 1818[†] records that

> The Timber now growing on the commonable lands called Malvern Chase within the said parish shall be fallen to defray the Expences of the foregoing alterations in and about the said Church … provided that the consent of the Lord of the Manor shall be first obtained in writing.

Vestry books contain minutes of meetings when parish officials discussed and decided upon matters of parochial importance – the vestry was thus the forerunner of parish councils which are civil institutions introduced in 1894. The name is derived from the fact that originally these meetings were held in the vestry or even in the church itself. When feelings ran high, however, there occurred scenes which were hardly appropriate in the church, so a change of venue became desirable, and many meetings were held in the village inn or, if there was one, in the school-room. The minutes give vivid and sometimes unexpected detail about rural life. Parishioners were rewarded for catching vermin, being given a penny or two for a 'hoop' (a bullfinch, one of numerous birds which decimated crops) or an 'urchin' (a hedgehog, believed to spoil milk by sucking from cows) or sparrows. A fox was worth about six times more than these smaller pests. Perhaps there was some scepticism as to the tales told by those seeking these bounties: in March 1741 Castlemorton

> agreed that no Hoops, Urchins or other vermin except foxes only shall ever be paid for hereafter.[‡]

---

* R.C. Gaut, *A History of Worcestershire Agriculture*, 1939, p.119.
† WRO BA 9581/19.
‡ *ibid.*

In the 18th century Castlemorton regularly spent a shilling (5p) a year 'suppressing the wake', an attempt to stop the over exuberant (and probably inappropriate) jollifications which often accompanied the celebration of Holy days or Saints days. Edwin Lees, who disapproved of wakes, wrote that they were 'usually observed on the Sunday next after the saint's day to whom the church was dedicated'.[*]

In the early 19th century Welland seems to have instituted the post of hayward to supervise its common, thus emphasising parochial ownership rather than the intercommoning of the chase era. Welland Vestry books show that his salary in 1830 was £28, in return for which he was to

> drive and keep off all cattle, horses, sheep, pigs and animals of every other denomination not belonging to the said parish.[†]

He had to impound stray animals and 'have them regularly cried at the nearest market towns and parish churches.' He was also to impound all

> scabby sheep horses and cattle ... and give the earliest information of all sheep that have got the maggot and all cattle needing the bull to their respective owners [and] prevent all persons picking up and carrying away dung or manure from the said common and to prevent ... parishioners from taking furze or gorze from off the said common and to give intelligence of all fresh encroachments upon the said common or waste lands in the parish of Welland.

Welland limited the number of animals allowed on its common by having a stint, which made clear to each commoner how many animals he might put out to graze. The hayward was to take

> care that no freeholder or commoner turns out more stock than they are entitled to do by Mr John Fletcher's Stint which was confirmed at Worcester Assizes August 1829.

In 1845 the hayward's 'exersion in detecting the person' earned him an extra half a crown (12½p) – the sum the parish had fined George Ganderton of Hanley Castle for taking turf from Welland Common.

There was another issue, resolution of which was to take many years – encroachment. The most blatant encroachment was when squatters set themselves up in hovels on common land and sat out the opposition. In 1721 Welland parish officials had referred to 'the pilfering brood' who seem to have set up their shacks on the wasteland. More subtle encroachment was when – apparently quite respectable – occupiers of property adjacent to the common surreptitiously took in a few yards at a time. It was easily done – gradually incorporating into their holding land adjacent to their boundary hedge on which they had left timber or agricultural equipment. If such activity was not challenged – and few could face the trouble and expense of legal action to do so – the land and its benefits were lost forever by the community. When land was plentiful and the population was small, this caused very little concern. Indeed, some encroachment on the wasteland was clearly tolerated or even encouraged. Welland parish officials

---

* Edwin Lees, *Pictures of Nature*, 1856, p.323.
† WRO BA 6359:850 and Pamela Hurle, *Beneath the Malvern Hills*, 1973, pp.26-7.

passed resolutions to 'cut up all encroachments that are not paid', implying that, if individuals were prepared to pay some acknowledgement, their taking in of a bit of common land was acceptable – in fact their payment may have been a welcome addition to parish finances. Similarly, although Castlemorton officials[*] required encroachers

> to throw up their fences and lay open to the common such encroachments and inclosures so that the commoners may enjoy their right of common without hindrance or molestation,

encroachment might be permitted, as in Welland, if the encroachers were

> willing to pay to the Parish an annual rent for such inclosure – the same may be received from such party with the full understanding that such payment is in satisfaction to the Parish for the Herbage annually accruing on such inclosures and which by having inclosed the land is lost to Commoners.

As the population increased, however, attitudes were to change and in some places encroachment could dramatically change the appearance of an area. Lords of the manor could actually derive considerable benefit from such encroachment. There is, however, some ambiguity in events in Great Malvern in 1806 when Andrew Foley, whose family had owned the manor of Malvern since 1741, started 20 different legal actions in one day against encroachers. He won 17 of the actions and, according to a handbill now in the hands of Malvern Hills Conservators, then claimed 'the different premises as his own', demonstrating that as lord of the manor he had

> the exclusive Right to the Commonable Lands, and had the full Power to inclose any Part He chose, without concurrence of the Freeholders and Commoners.

Other evidence in the Conservators' possession suggests that he did this 'for the purpose of again throwing open the same'. Three of the actions were successfully defended, enabling their occupants to stay put, one of them being the lawyer Philip Ballard, father of Stephen Ballard of Colwall, who was vociferously to criticise Lady Emily Foley half a century later. For by the middle of the 19th century the Foley lords of the manor of Malvern, far from opposing encroachment and house building at Link Top, charged the occupants modest sums as acknowledgement that an encroachment had been made with the manorial lord's blessing. This extended the Foley empire and led to the, at first derisory, nickname of Newtown for the development. Although the likes of Stephen Ballard, who had spent countless happy boyhood hours roaming the common surrounding his home at Link Top, were unhappy about this, the Foleys were merely exercising a manorial right which had existed since the 1235 Statute of Merton: provided the wasteland was not actually needed for grazing, the lord could legally allow it to be used for other purposes. It was called approving the common. Some lawyers believed the Statute of Merton to be obsolete, although nationally lords of manors successfully contended that their various uses of common land were perfectly justifiable under its terms.[†] Some local inhabitants regarded the whole business as theft, summed up in a popular piece of doggerel:

---

* WRO 9581/19.
† Lord Eversley, *Commons, Forests and Footpaths*, 1910, pp.9-14.

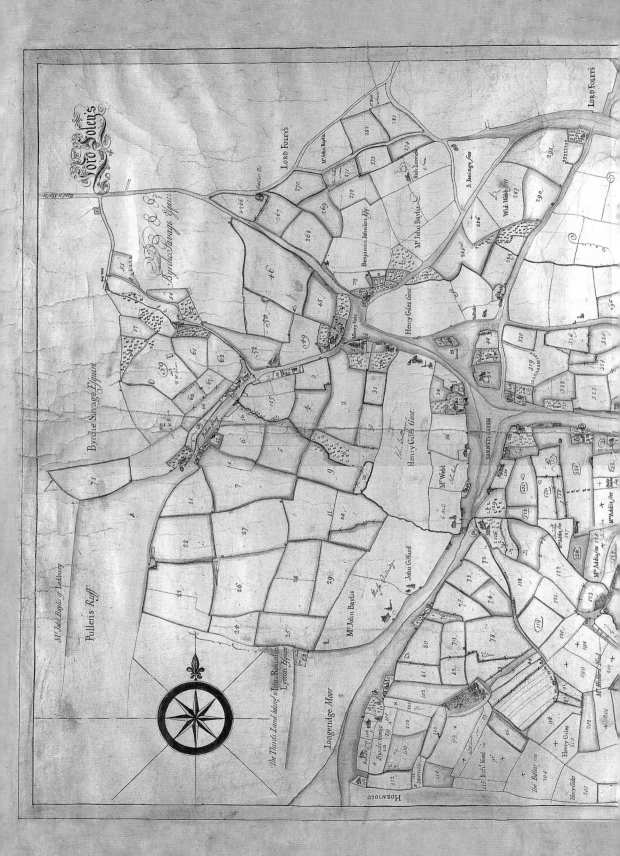

Map the First, contains all that Part of The Manor of MUCH MALVERN bounded on the North by SHERARDS GREEN &c. and on the South by Bleakmoor Park and part of the CHACE The Property of Lord Foley.

BLEAKMOOR PARK in the Parish of Hanley Castle and Chacery of Worcester the Property of John Hornold Esquire

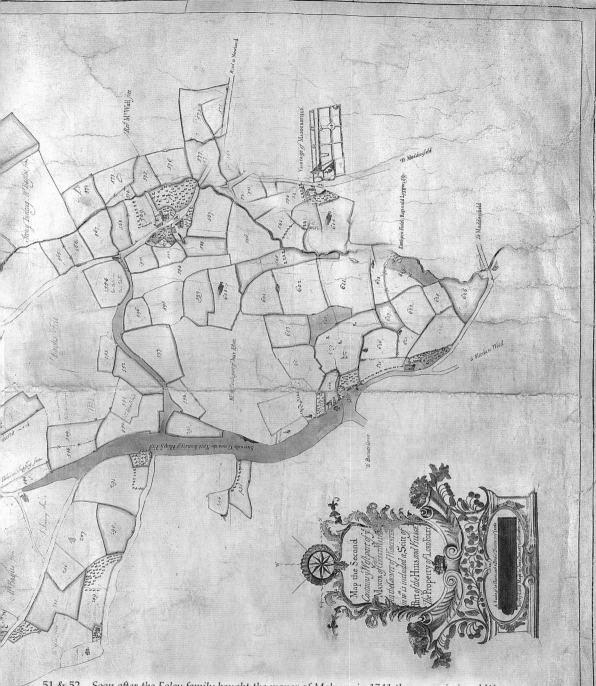

51 & 52   Soon after the Foley family bought the manor of Malvern in 1741 they commissioned Worcestershire's leading mapmaker, John Doharty, to produce maps of the area. These maps were mislaid for many years but are now in Worcestershire Record Office, deposited by the Malvern Hills Conservators, who bought the manor (and hence the maps) from the Foley family in 1925. The uncoloured copies made for Malvern Library are familiar to several generations of visitors to the Library's Malvern Room, but the colour and detail of the originals show the reasons for the Doharty family's high reputation.

> The law will punish man or woman
> Who steals a goose from off the common;
> But lets the greater felon loose,
> Who steals the common off the goose.

Documents in Upton-upon-Severn's records show what expectations people had from proper use of common land – and also how concerned leading parishioners were to prevent abuses. Manorial courts were usually held twice a year to deal with petty crime (at the Court Leet) and administration of the manor, its land and property rights (at the Court Baron). Upton

> is a large parish containing 8 or 10 miles in circumference, having many Freeholders, Coppiholders and Leaseholders. In it are very large commonable meadows and pastures over and above several hundreds of acres of wast commons. ... All persons inhabiting within ye Parish and having a house or land claim a right of communing in ye said meadows and pastures. ... There is a Court Leet and Baron held by the Lord of the Manor at one of which formerly have been made Bylaws and Ordinances for regulating ye said commons, some for restraining ye sorts of cattle to be putt in and ye time when; some for keeping up particular portions of the said commonable meadows and pastures ... in such manner and stint as 6 chosen at ye court shall appoint; some for laying pains upon such as stock with more than they can winter. ...This power of making Bylaws and Ordinances not having for many years been putt in execution and no distress taken for breach of them is now thought not sufficient.
>
> By reason of the great encouragement from ye commons multitudes of Poor are tempted to settle in ye parish and are now so burthensome yt the parishioners pay near 3ˢ in ye pound to ye poors levy. ...
>
> In regard of this and that the said commons are ... of little benefit to the several landholders of the Parish the Lord of the Manor and the Generality of the persons interested are inclined to apply for an Act of Parliament to give a Power to regulate their commons and to make such Bylaws and Ordinances relating to them as shall be thought convenient for the support of the Poor or other publick use of ye parish with sufficient power to compel performance.
>
> Or to inclose part of the wast commons to be applyd to public use.
>
> Or for others to inclose by consent of a majority. [*]

Upton did not enclose until the mid-19th century, but this document leads us to consider an additional anxiety about the loss of common rights as a result of enclosure, about which confusion often arises as it can mean two very different processes. Enclosure can refer to the consolidation of strips held since medieval times in the communally farmed arable fields: in order that individual farmers might farm more efficiently by holding all their land as fairly compact estates they might exchange land with neighbours and fence it off. This had been done quite amicably since Tudor times. But enclosure can also – much more controversially – mean the incorporation of former wasteland, on which many people enjoyed valuable rights, into the privately-owned sector.

Upton contained

> several large meadows and pastures ... in which severall have distinct property or parcels of land all or most of which meadows and pastures are common either when the Hay is cut and carried off or at Lammas and such in the Parish who have a house or house and land ... have a right of communing in such meadows or

---

[*] WRO 705:46 104/4.

pastures. There are likewise … severall large fields of arable land in which severall have property. The custom in those fields … as are not enclosed to plow two years and fallow the third, and such parts of those common fields as are not enclosed when fallow as well as after the corn is cut have been open to the commoners. But it has been a custom in the Parish for 40, 50, 60 years or more for persons having parcels of grounds in these fields lyeing convenient together to enclose them and keep them severall all the year. This they have done for many years and are so doing every year and it is presumed most of the Parish was open till by Degrees thus enclosed. And some Grounds are now open which were formerly enclosed as appears by the hedges round now standing.

The persons of small property in the parish oppress the commons by putting in large stocks of Cattle more than they can keep in the winter … or great numbers of sheep and for such purpose insisting that there is no sett stint they are at liberty to put in as many as they please.

When 'the Lord and the most substantial Freeholders, being willing to put a stop to this and to bring the commoners to a reasonable stock', raised a number of queries, the answers made it absolutely clear that commoners regarded all and any enclosures in the common fields as unlawful and intended to 'throw them down at the open time of year when the rest of the field is open'. The central issue is that all enclosure necessarily involves the rights and property of people who often have conflicting interests. The Upton landowners, shown above to be interested in the possibility of enclosure, would not find it easy. Even enclosing the communally held arable fields could pose problems.

For many years farmers who wished to enclose had to obtain the passage of a special Act through parliament to achieve their end, though an Act in 1836 allowed enclosure without a specific Act if two-thirds of the owners of two-thirds of the common arable fields agreed. In 1845 matters were further simplified by allowing a body of Enclosure Commissioners to supervise the process.

Enclosure of the wasteland was even more complex than that of the common arable fields, especially in an area where intercommoning had occurred, as it did in Malvern Chase. Intercommoning in the chase meant that the rights which had to be taken into consideration were not merely those of parishioners in a single parish but also those of claimants from all the other parishes which had enjoyed common rights on the wasteland of the chase. Those rights had been guaranteed in perpetuity by the 17th-century disafforestation decree. Of the parishes recognised as having been in Malvern Chase, some were particularly vociferous whenever enclosure was mooted. It is surprising that eventually their objections were overridden, as this chapter now describes.

Enclosure was, and is, a subject that divides historians, their views coloured by their political leanings. It is, however, fair to say that if the rich and influential wanted enclosure it took place, regardless of the views and interests of the poor and impotent. Enclosure offered new opportunities for the larger or more efficient farmer to increase the yield and quality of his crops, meat, wool, dairy produce and so on, thus improving food supplies. The population of England increased dramatically in the 18th century, and experimental methods were devised, aimed at maximising yields and improving quality in both arable and stock farming. Influential large landowners sought not only to consolidate sometimes scattered estates but also to bring into private ownership the wasteland on which it was uneconomic to leave their animals. They wanted to segregate their animals in order to try to avoid their catching the diseases which were rife when all sorts and conditions of beasts mingled together. They also wanted to try out new selective breeding programmes and new rotations of crops. None of this was practicable without enclosure so they naturally supported parliamentary enclosure acts enabling them to bring into private ownership land which from time immemorial had been enjoyed by all freeholders and tenants communally.

But enclosure inevitably caused distress to poorer people who lost common rights they had enjoyed for centuries. As Arthur Young's poor labourer put it,

> Parliament may be tender of property: all I know is that I had a cow and an Act of Parliament has taken it from me.[*]

In lieu of common rights, land was distributed in proportion to one's property, so the rich were awarded large allotments and the poor were given small portions which they often could not afford to fence. The usual method of enclosure, using hawthorn or quick, is described by William Pitt who surveyed Worcestershire Agriculture and reported his findings to the Board of Agriculture which operated from 1793 until 1823. He quotes a farmer, Mr Pomeroy:

> The new fences are chiefly made with hawthorn, secured by post and rails ... The expense of making them is difficult to judge of with accuracy; but from the supply of materials, which are in most parts plentiful, it may be deemed moderate.[†]

When Charles I took his third of the wasteland within Malvern Chase the disafforestation decree promised that the remaining two-thirds would be left open and free in perpetuity. Despite this undertaking, parliamentary enclosure occurred here in the late 18th century. Leigh, in 1776, and Hanley Castle, in 1795, were the first parishes to secure the enclosure acts enabling them to enclose the former waste. The passing of these two acts seems to have involved astonishing legal sleight of hand. As Cora Weaver has noted,[‡] no mention was made in either of them of the promises made in the disafforestation decree. Had Parliament been alerted to this, or even to the fact of the land having once comprised part of a chase, the bills may not have been so obligingly passed by Parliament.

There were immense legal and practical complications when these two parishes enclosed wasteland in the former chase. Men from the numerous other chase parishes that had enjoyed valuable rights, through the practice of intercommoning since time immemorial, became very angry indeed. The countryman jealously guards rights attached to land. Posts and rails enclosing the Leigh enclosures were removed almost as soon as they were put up in January 1778. 'Malicious and evil disposed persons ... did pull up and prostrate some posts and rails, and quick, set up and planted upon part of the Link Common,' piling and firing them upon a piece of land enclosed by Sir Charles Cocks. Despite threats of punishment, certain persons in November of the same year

> did feloniously appear on the High Road; and upon the uninclosed part of the Link ... with their faces blackened, and being otherwise disguised, and armed with guns and other offensive weapons; and in the most daring manner did cut down, burn and entirely destroy all the posts, gates and rails' erected in accordance with the Act.[§]

---

[*] Arthur Young, *A Six Month Tour through the North of England*, 1770.
[†] William Pitt, *A General View of the Agriculture of the County of Worcester*, 1813, p.58.
[‡] Cora Weaver, *Forest Law, Custom and Enclosure of Malvern Chase 1776-1884*, 1995, pp.10,11,16.
[§] R.C. Gaut, *A History of Worcestershire Agriculture*, 1939, p.163, quoting a newspaper source.

53 *This stone, by the porch of Berrow Church, commemorates the murder of the Gummary family in May 1780 soon after the enclosure of Leigh.*

The episode was followed by mysterious and particularly gruesome murders in 1780, when four people were bludgeoned and hacked to death as they lay in bed in Berrow. The mystery was eventually solved when one of the guilt-ridden perpetrators confessed on his death-bed many years later. The murders were revenge against one of the victims, believed to have been tempted by a promised reward to give the authorities information about the fence breakers.[*]

Implementation of the Leigh Enclosure Act may have proved dramatically difficult, but it did not deter Hanley Castle from getting its Act passed nearly 20 years later. The longstanding Hornyold interest in Hanley Castle remained very strong and, with the Church and the Lechmere family, the Hornyold family was a major beneficiary of the 1795 legislation. It benefited again when a second Hanley Enclosure Act in 1817 enabled the Hornyolds to absorb into their estates the 98 acres of common which had been retained for the benefit of cottagers in 1795. Comparison of Isaac Taylor's 1772 map of Worcestershire with that of Christopher Greenwood in 1822 shows how dramatically enclosure could change the appearance of a parish. The inter-commoning issue meant that Hanley Castle faced legal challenges from Colwall, Mathon and Malvern men seeking to pre-serve their perceived rights. Despite spending large sums of money on fees to lawyers to challenge this view, Hanley Castle was forced to make allotments of land to Colwall and Mathon to compensate for their loss of common rights.[†]

The legal and financial complications may have deterred other parishes from enclosure of wasteland for half a century, though a bill was prepared in 1814 when the lords of other chase parishes proposed a general enclosure of former chase wasteland. However,

> Lord Somers addressed the lords of manors and proprietors of freeholds on Malvern Chace, announcing his intention of giving up all further attempts to bring about enclosure of the same. He found it impossible to reconcile so many conflicting interests.[‡]

* WRO 6218/7.
† Percival Birkett, *Malvern Hills, Historical Sketch compiled from Public Records and County Histories, with observations*, 1882, p.15.
‡ T.C. Turberville, *Worcestershire in the 19th century*, p.243.

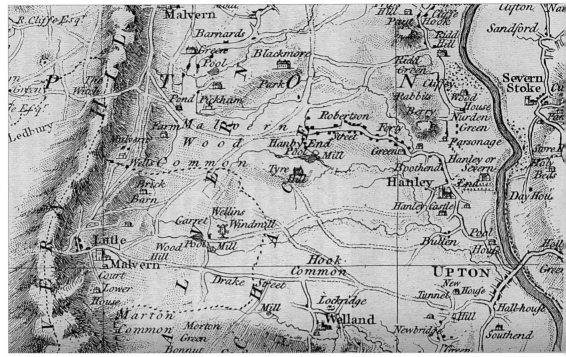

54   *Part of Isaac Taylor's 1772 map of Worcestershire showing Hanley Castle before its enclosure.*

This is not surprising. Families with manorial interests included the Foleys in Great Malvern, Mary Wakeman (succeeded by her Berington relations) in Little Malvern, the Martins in Upton, William Thackwell in Birtsmorton, Robert Higgins in Berrow and Pitt-Browne in Bromsberrow. As if this were not enough the Dean and Chapter of Westminster held Mathon, Longdon and Castlemorton (the two latter being let out to the Dowdeswells) while the Bishop of Worcester held Welland and the Bishop of Hereford held Colwall. All were accustomed to doing things their way.

Malvern's early historian, John Chambers, confirmed that

> Lord Somers suggested and took some pains to promote an inclosure of the waste lands in Mathon, Colwall and the adjoining parishes, which his Lordship proposed doing as a public benefit, but from the variety of claims, the perplexity of boundaries, and probable litigation likely to ensue, he was induced to abandon his plan.[*]

Chambers also, however, referred to recent draining of part of the chase which had been

> covered with large sheets of water, the constant evaporation of which rendered the air blown from it upon Malvern damp and unwholesome.[†]

---

[*]   John Chambers, *A General History of Malvern*, 1817, p.143.
[†]   John Chambers, *ibid.*, p.144.

In addition to the legal costs of getting an enclosure act through parliament, implementing its provisions required professional surveying and laying out of plots, new roads and amenity areas. This did not come cheap. The whole process of enclosure was a lucrative seam for lawyers, surveyors and other professionals to mine. Nash, always a shrewd observer, saw what was happening even before it reached its peak. He wrote in the late 18th century:

> Inclosures have been the fashion in Worcestershire as well as in other counties, though I much doubt whether they would so often have been applied for to parliament if the solicitors of the acts, surveyors, commissioners etc had not gained more money by them than the landholders and tenants.[*]

The late 18th and early 19th centuries saw agricultural change when food prices, rents and land values increased – at serious cost to the labouring classes, whose wages did not rise in proportion. It was also a time of huge increases in poor rates, well illustrated by former chase parishes. Welland's costs in maintaining its poor rose from nearly £108 in 1792 to £393 in 1801, reaching a record £510 in 1819.[†] Hanley Castle's rose from £350 in 1788-9 to £1,526 in 1832-3.[‡]

---

[*] T.R. Nash, *Worcestershire*, Vol. I, p.xi.
[†] Pamela Hurle, *Beneath the Malvern Hills*, 1973, p.49.
[‡] Pamela Hurle, *Hanley Castle, Heart of Malvern Chase*, 1978, p.122.

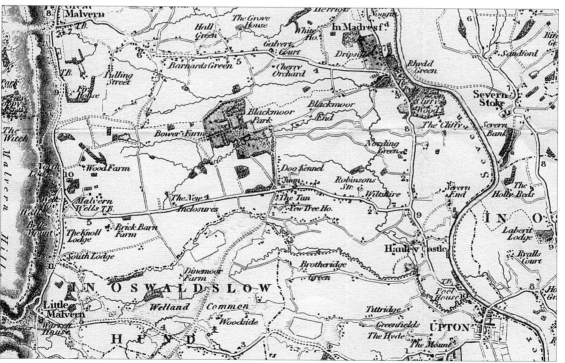

55 *Part of Christopher Greenwood's 1822 map of Worcestershire showing the effects of enclosure on Hanley Castle. 'The new enclosures' are marked, as are new roads, driven straight through the former Malvern Wood Common.*

Agricultural societies began to be formed in the late 18th century. The present Three Counties Society was formed in 1922 when the societies of Herefordshire (founded 1797), Worcestershire (1816) and Gloucestershire (1829) amalgamated. When the individual societies were first formed, their annual one-day shows were held, for example, in Broad Street, in the heart of the county town of Hereford. Whilst such an event would be unthinkable in today's sanitised and traffic-laden streets, the early 19th-century inhabitants of any town would have been quite accustomed to seeing all kinds of animals in the streets. Not only were they employed to pull carts and wagons —it was common to see pigs roaming about and rooting among the rubbish and rotting vegetable matter to be found in any market town before refuse collection and street cleaning became the norm, paid for out of the rates.

As set out by the Herefordshire Society in its early catalogues, the aims of agricultural societies included:

- To promote the knowledge of agriculture by encouraging experiments ... and by distributing rewards to such perons as shall produce the best and most abundant crops of grain and grass in proportion to the quality of the land they occupy.
- To encourage the improvement of waste and other lands by enclosing, draining and manuring in the most cheap and effectual manner.
- To promote all improvements in the several implements now used by the farmers here, and to introduce such new ones as experience has proven to be of value elsewhere ...
- To ascertain and make public the best means of raising and protecting orchards, of propagating the best fruits; and the most easy and certain efficacious manner of proceeding in all the stages of manufacturing their produce into cider and jelly.
- To encourage industry and fidelity among servants employed in husbandry.
- To reward labourers who shall bring up, or have already brought up the greatest number of legitimate children, without any or with smallest relief from their respective parishes.*

This last aim involved a prize of 12 guineas (£12.60p) – fabulous wealth to a labourer earning a few shillings a week. Today, a time when families tend to be small, it might strike us as somewhat bizarre, but becomes rather more understandable when we recall that farmers wanted plentiful, cheap labour. At the same time parish officials wanted to keep as low as possible the demands made on property owners for the rates which helped the poor. Due to the so-called Speenhamland System, devised at the end of the 18th century, some unscrupulous farmers paid low wages in the knowledge that labourers could get them supplemented out of the poor rates – in effect getting a subsidy for their wages bills out of the rates. Such a system was demoralising for the labourer forced to go cap in hand to the parish overseers and, although there is no firm evidence that it happened in the former chase parishes, it seems very likely. Certainly, as we have seen, poor rates did rise here at the time when the Speenhamland System was adopted in many parishes throughout the country.

The early agricultural shows were particularly exciting affairs, but people regularly went to market towns such as Upton and Ledbury to buy and sell

---

* quoted by Glynne Hastings, Secretary of the Three Counties Agricultural Society from 1946 to 1972, in the 1976 Show catalogue, pp.7-11.

goods and, at the less frequent 'mop fairs', to find work or hire workers. Directly or indirectly about half the population of Worcestershire earned its living from agriculture in the first part of the 19th century. A labouring father's low wages were often supplemented by mother's earnings from home work such as glove-making in such time as the poor woman could find among her other numerous duties. Her prime task was to rear children – sometimes large numbers of them – who might also earn a few pence from odd jobs or picking berries and flowers to sell in the nearest town.

William Howitt in 1838 vividly – perhaps romantically – described market day.[*]

> Howitt and many others have picturesquely described scenes on the roads on the mornings of fair-days and market days, the business transacted, and the return home at night. The foot-paths filled with a succession of pedestrians, men and women, with baskets on their arms ... The carriage road equally alive with people riding and driving – farmers, country gentlemen, parish overseers – drawn by some real or imaginary business and rattling along on horseback, or in carriages of various kinds, gigs, spring-carts and carts without springs... .The carriers wagons and covered carts crowded with women, and dogs under the seats. In the afternoon and evening the same procession, but instead of farm produce the baskets and vehicles laden with household necessities. 'The farmers go riding and driving out three times as fast as they came, for they are primed with good dinners and strong beer.' Farmers and servants attended the 'mops'; ... the shepherd displayed a lock of wool in his hat, the milkmaid a tuft of cow-hair and the wagoner a whip-cord to denote the respective occupations. 'The farmers go amongst them, enquiring after their accomplishments and qualities, cheapening them as much as they would cheapen a horse and their no less wary wives negotiating with buxom damsels of the mop and pail. These matters all satisfactorily settled and the 'earnest' or money given on account of future services' the bargain was concluded.

The expanse between Malvern and Worcester – which included part of that surveyed by Dingley and his companions in 1584 – was described by a traveller taking the coach from the new railway station at Worcester in 1856.[†]

> The route lies through a track of land, perhaps as fertile as any in England, and which appears to be cultivated up to the highest remunerative point. Extensive orchards line the road for a considerable distance – orchards which are corn-fields as well; for beneath the apple trees stand golden crops of grain, of oats, of barley, of wheat, almost ready to the sickle. Then there are fields of hops and rich pasture lands, and anon we come upon a huge track [sic] planted with the famous Barham pear trees – trees as big as average elms, and yielding in immeasurable quantities the small juicy pear from which is brewed the famous perry of the district.

Potential profits for go-ahead farmers meant that many places in Worcester-shire had been enclosed – Gaut lists over 50 enclosure acts between 1795 and 1819.[‡] But, as we have seen, in the former chase parishes high legal costs and conflicting interests seem to have deferred further enclosure until the middle of the century.

---

[*] quoted and commented on by R.C. Gaut, *A History of Worcestershire Agriculture*, 1939, p.255.
[†] *The Leisure Hour*, 1856, p.698.
[‡] R.C.Gaut, *op.cit.*, pp.217-8.

The climate of opinion had changed by the mid-19th century, when there was a flurry of enclosure legislation in the period sometimes referred to as the 'Golden Age' of agriculture. In 1845 Castlemorton, Birtsmorton and Longdon went in for enclosure with rather less zeal than Hanley Castle, not facing up to the challenge of sorting out grazing rights. They clarified ownership and con-solidated holdings in arable fields but left extensive areas of wasteland intact so that large tracts were left in a condition reminiscent of how it must have looked in the Middle Ages. Castlemorton Common was not, and is not, densely covered in trees, but consists largely of open scrubland with a wide variety of plant and animal life which must have delighted Worcestershire naturalists who founded their field club in 1847. There were other limits, too: as William Pitt[*] wrote, the upper parts of

> Malvern Hill ... being rocky, are generally impracticable for cultivation and must therefore ever remain sheep walk or plantation.

Enclosure acts set aside a few acres for parish purposes. Welland's 1852 enclosure of its arable and waste, for example, earmarked one acre as a burial ground (which was not actually used until nearly a hundred years later). Three acres became 'a place of exercise and recreation for the inhabitants'. In addition, a field was to be divided into allotments 'for the labouring poor'. This enabled them to grow vegetables, but there was no longer any common land on which to graze their animals. The allotments were clearly a sop to those who condemned the enclosure, recognising it as beneficial to the rich but disastrous for those to whom common rights were a significant part of their means of subsistence. Opposition from other chase parishes, which in the light of earlier history was only to be expected, actually came to nothing.

When the common disappeared there were more subtle losses, as Edwin Lees noted in the mid-1850s:

> Welland Common, which long remained a waste, included in the old Malvern Chase, intersected with a devious brook curling through its hollows, used to nour-ish some curious and local plants, which I am afraid will now be sought in vain there since the enclosure; for even Garret Pool has been much circumscribed, if not quite destroyed.[†]

John Rayer Lane of Castlemorton left diaries packed with information on farming life from the 1820s until his death in 1871. On his farms in and around Castlemorton and Eastnor, he employed up to 16 labourers, producing large quantities of cheese, cider and perry, as well as keeping sheep and other animals. At the end of 1845 he observed that farm labourers 'were never more employed, and at good wages too'. By 1850 he reverted to his customarily more cautious comment and, although he often took a broad national view in his comments, may have been reflecting the effects of enclosure in the former chase parishes:

> The energies of the British Farmer were never more applied than at the present time altho the price of produce is so ruinously low. There is generally more money expended on the land in draining grubbing trees stocking fences etc ... than I ever remember before

* William Pitt, *op.cit.*, p.188.
† Edwin Lees, *Pictures of Nature in the Silurian Region around the Malvern Hills*, 1856, p.84.

56 & 57   *The Guarlford Road and old cottages at Guarlford. When much of the Foley Estate was sold in 1910 the sale catalogue included pictures such as these.*

58 & 59   *Old cottages at Guarlford and Sherrards Green, where a pair of semi-detached cottages set in nearly an acre of ground brought in a rent of £14 a year. Described as old in 1910, such cottages would have been typical of forest homes serving many generations of locals.*

It is indicative of the high regard in which Lane was held that in 1856 he was elected unopposed as valuer and surveyor for Upton's enclosure process. An honest and honourable man, with a dry humour and canny ability to sum up humans as well as animals, he had no illusions about the work and temptations facing those who implemented enclosure:

> I hope and trust that at the finish of this arduous and responsible undertaking I may deserve as much popularity as I seem now to have.*

Berrow enclosed in 1860, Upton in 1863 and Longdon in 1872. Longdon at last drained its marsh which had been the subject of debate for over a hundred years. James Brindley, the famous engineer, had himself surveyed it in 1763 but nothing came of it.† Edwin Lees, leading light of the Malvern and Worcestershire Naturalists Clubs, described it as

> one of the most singular spots in Worcestershire ... surrounded on all sides by deep ditches, and tenanted principally by flocks of geese. [It is] a barren space ... In dry seasons some adventurous borderer fences in a portion ... and perhaps next year ... the farm labourers have to mow the grass up to their knees in water, or are unable to mow it at all; and thus it is left, a harsh autumnal fodder for rough colts and broken-down horses. ‡

In the glory days of farming employers entertained their workers, as recalled by the daughter of Stephen Ballard, leading landowner in Colwall:§

> What an event was the Harvest Home Supper every Autumn, held in the granaries of the Winnings Farm at 6 o'clock. The guests, some 300, arrived and sat down to a real English dinner of roast and boiled beef and mutton, plum pudding, apple pies and rice pudding. Then came the toasts to Queen Victoria, and the British Work-man, followed by a talk by father generally on 'thrift'. At 9 o'clock the tables were removed and dancing began. The first was a country dance called 'The Triumph' led off by father and Mrs Bright – and Trimbell, the bricklayer and his wife. ... Only one year did we exceed the time of closing (12 o'clock) because my father's watch had stopped.

By the last quarter of the 19th century serious concern was being expressed at the large-scale erosion of the common land which had been promised in perpetuity to local freeholders and tenants. To add insult to injury, most of it had been lost through enclosure, which was perfectly legal because it had parliamentary blessing. Edwin Lees pleaded that there might be left around Malvern

> a few green slopes ... and the beauteous hills at any rate remain in the grassy and mossy investiture they have derived from the careless but graceful hand of nature.¶

---

*   Pamela Hurle, *Castlemorton Farmer, John Rayer Lane*, 1996, p.46.
†   *Victoria History of the County of Worcestershire*, Vol. IV, p.111.
‡   Edwin Lees, *Pictures of Nature*, 1856, p.87.
§   Ada Ballard's memories, private property of the Ballard family.
¶   Edwin Lees, *The Forest and Chace of Malvern*, 1877, p.57.

XIII

Visitors and the Growing Need
for Conservation

Encroachment and enclosure were not the only reasons for concern in 19th-century Malvern. As early as 1824 complaint* was made about

great damage ... done to the young trees planted for the sake of ornament on part of Malvern Hill by Donkeys being turned thereon by Persons having no right to do so. And also great inconvenience arises to the Public by a great number of Donkeys for hire being placed in the middle of the Highway in the height of the Malvern Summers Season.

A few years later prints published by Henry Lamb, who kept the Royal Library in the building now used by Barclays Bank, also show the popularity of donkeys, which carried less energetic visitors up the hills and provided a livelihood for some of the poorer inhabitants of the village. John Chambers[†] noted that those too timid to ride a donkey could hire a donkey cart:

The owners of Jerusalem ponies ply for hire: here are also to be let Donkey carts, where patrons of the whip may drive these animals curricle or tandem.

---

* From documents in the possession of Malvern Hills Conservators.
† John Chambers, *A General History of Malvern*, 1817, p.93.

60 *Most donkey proprietors were women, described by a writer in* The Leisure Hour *of 1862 as 'of the softer sex who drive the hardest bargains'. They employed boys and girls to look after the donkeys and escort them up and down the hills when people hired them for a few pence. This is a 19th-century print.*

61   *A flattering view of Belle Vue Terrace and Island.*

Summer visitors and provision for their enjoyment were, however, perceived by local commoners as incompatible with historic rights on Malvern's commons and hillsides – hence the grumble about damage to trees and the assertion that donkey owners had no right to turn their animals on to the hills. Holders of ancient rights resented others trying to usurp them. Such early references to both donkeys and a summer season in Malvern indicate that it was becoming a fashionable resort – indeed, the young Princess Victoria came in 1830 with her mother, the Duchess of Kent. Their visit gave rise to the name of Victoria Drive, leading to the house in which they stayed – Holly Mount. The house was demolished in the late 19th century, about the same time as the building of the non-conformist Holly Mount Church.

The Foley family, who had bought the manor of Malvern in 1741, were amongst the first to recognise commercial value in making the village of Malvern attractive to visitors. In the employ of Edward Foley, architects and builders began to beautify the unappealing northern entrance to Malvern in the 1820s.[*] Samuel Deykes started a small library, enlarged by John Southall, whose wife Mary, plagiarising contemporary work such as John Chambers' *History of Malvern*, wrote a guide-book which was re-issued several times in the 1820s. The Library House was renamed the Royal Library, presumably in honour of the visit of Princess Victoria and her mother in 1830. It is an eye-catching end-piece to the range of buildings completed in the 1820s to provide the 'commodious and elegant' baths and pump room close to the very successful *Foley Arms Hotel* built in 1810 and named by its proprietor John Downs in honour of the lord of the manor. One of the most dramatic developments of hillside land was the setting

---

[*]   Bills and accounts are in Hereford Record Office.

out of the appropriately named Belle Vue Terrace with an attractive island of
land below the terrace instead of the then existing rather scruffy junction with
Church Street. It was proposed to create

> a new feature of elegant and comprehensive beauty... .The prettiest part of Mal-
> vern is perhaps the line above the church, where the Belle Vue Hotel is situated. ...
> Proceeding thence, along the road to Hereford, there is a very considerable curve
> to the right, and the road thereafter assumes a convex form round the base of the
> hills. ... The suggestion is, to erect a rough parapet wall at certain given points,
> to fill up the chasm from the hills, level with the present road, by which a most
> enchanting line of straight and level carriage-drive would be made, directly into
> Malvern, and the curve in which the road now runs might be appropriated to villas
> or a crescent. The situation would be exquisite and, as a promenade and drive it
> would be unequalled, both in respect to its altitude and command of scenery.[*]

*   Mary Southall, *A Description of Malvern*, 1822, pp.58-9.

62 *Maria Martin's early
19th-century view of Malvern.*

63 *Fashionable visitors to the
Chalybeate Spa Cottage.*

64 *Although this print of the Holy Well dates from the middle of the 19th century, it was attracting large numbers of visitors in the late 18th century. Now known as Malvern Wells, the area was originally part of the extensive parish of Hanley Castle, one of whose main landowners was the Hornyold family. Considerable building took place in Malvern Wells in the 19th century.*

65 *This print shows St Ann's well-house in 1860, and includes some of the donkeys which became a popular subject for prints and postcards. The Victorians added a mushroom-like building on the left to cater for increased numbers of visitors, several of whom are depicted walking on the hills and on the paths around the well-house.*

As the tourist industry so genteelly dawned, Malvern had numerous bene-factors whose names were given to paths on the hills, the construction of some of which they financed. The precise nature of their generosity has been lost in the mists of time, but their names appeared on 19th-century maps and included Buchanan's Walk, Damer's Walk and Merrick's Walk, while the steep slope from Church Street up to the Royal Library rejoiced in the name Paradise Row.

For those unhappy about sharing the attractions of Malvern with summer visitors much worse was to come. From 1842 the insignificant village of Malvern was transformed into a fashionable little spa town, the number of visitors hugely increasing with the building in the early 1860s of railway stations in Malvern Link Great Malvern and, later, Malvern Wells. Excursion trains turned the Malvern Hills into a playground for Black Country workers and others whose humdrum lives were much improved by the opportunity to escape for a day out.

The medieval balance of power between the constituent parishes of the chase was also changing. Hanley Castle, the old seat of administration and a large parish, had become rather a rural backwater. Nevertheless, since Malvern Wells

66   *St Ann's Well in the early 20th century.*

67   *Malvern Link Station has been sadly treated, and the nearby hotel, which was a boys' preparatory school for much of its life, was destroyed in the 1960s to make way for modern apartments.*

was within its boundaries, there were valuable plots of land, largely owned by the Hornyold family, ripe for development. Malvern never had a market like that in Upton but its provision of visitor facilities – hotels, boarding houses, shops, library, concert hall and churches – eventually led to it usurping Upton's historic position at the centre of things. For example, in 1836 a Union Workhouse to serve Upton and the surrounding 21 parishes including Malvern, was built in Upton. By 1894, when local government reform took place, Malvern headed an urban district council, whereas Upton became the centre of a rural district council. It was the urban district council which survived 20th-century local government changes, and implemented policies which Uptonians resented. These included the removal of administrative offices from Upton and the 1980 demolition of the old workhouse, a building for which people in Upton had some affection and many plans for its future use.

The first significant contributors to Malvern's commercial success were the doctors who specialised in hydrotherapy. Led by Dr James Wilson and Dr James Manby Gully, they saw that water from springs on the Malvern Hills could enable the establishment of a spa comparable with those in continental Europe. Dr Wilson had visited that at Graefenberg in Austrian Silesia, been entranced by the work there of Vincent Priessnitz and determined to turn Malvern into an English Graefenberg. Aided by the natural beauty of the Malvern landscape and establishing their practices on the properties of Malvern water, they turned the village into a health resort, where shopkeepers, hoteliers and boarding-house keepers could all make a comfortable living as they plied their respective trades. Even at six o'clock in the morning a band played at St Ann's Well where

68   *Opened in 1862 when the railway reached Great Malvern, in 1919 Elmslie's impressive* Imperial Hotel *became the main building of Malvern Girls' College and, after the 2006 amalgamation, Malvern St James.*

a number of persons were assembled around the well, sitting, standing or walking, but each and all occupied from time to time in drinking the water which trickles out of a marble mouth into a marble basin in a romantic little room. The whole of the surrounding hills were alive with people ... Far away, up to the heights of the Worcestershire Beacon...the entire of the slopes ... were thronged with multitudes seeking health, where health is truly to be found – from cold water, mountain breezes, and exercise.[*]

And the donkeys were certainly here to stay until the 1930s.

Why did the water doctors choose Malvern? Malvern had, since at least the 17th century, attracted people who believed in the curative powers of its water. Scientific analysis in 1757 by Dr John Wall, a versatile physician who helped to found both Worcester Infirmary and the Worcester Porcelain Company, proved that Malvern water was exceptionally pure:

> 'The Malvern water', says Dr John Wall,
> 'Is famed for containing just nothing at all.'

The popularity of the Malvern water-cure was actually quite short-lived but gave a massive boost to visitor numbers which were also greatly increased by day trippers. This burgeoning tourism meant that 19th-century developments in the Malvern Chase area caused anxiety to owners of traditional common rights but offered commercial opportunity to all those catering for visitors. Although the motives of each group were in conflict with those of the other, they shared a common aim – to save the Malvern Hills. They began to publicise their concerns in the 1850s.

---

[*]   A Restored Invalid, *The Metropolis of the Water Cure*, 1858, pp.56-7.

69   *The view from the* Imperial Hotel *adjacent to Great Malvern Station.*

70 & 71   *The hills and woodland that had once provided sport for privileged medieval hunters came to be used by thousands of ordinary people for activities gently mocked by 19th-century cartoonists. The donkey featured in many cartoons.*

72 & 73   *A windy day, and a ride for more affluent visitors to the hills.*

One of the effects of the Malvern summer season was the establishment of a local newspaper – *The Malvern Advertiser*. In September 1858 it published a letter of complaint:

> Where is the pedestrian in Malvern, who, going up the Worcestershire Beacon has not met with a danger of a special kind? Who does not know how careful one must be before one indulges in a minute's rest on the soft slopes? There is a large piece of broken plate – there a threatening bit of a glass or a bottle. If it is not safe to sit down, one may easily conceive that it is far more dangerous to slide on the slopes; the pleasures of the children is [*sic*] therefore spoilt. But children are not the only ones fond of that sport, for grown-up people too (and why not?) like now and then to follow the example of their youngsters. Therefore many accidents of a dreadful character are to be feared.

This delightful picture of the supposedly staid Victorian middle-class also shows a feeling that the hills and commons needed somehow to be 'managed'. In 1858 a committee was appointed by freeholders, tenants and commoners to prevent encroachments. It proved to be too weak to challenge the influence of the Foley

74   *A romanticised mid-19th-century print of visitors enjoying the view at Malvern Wells.*

family, who, as lords of the manor of Malvern, were only too happy to permit encroachments if encroachers paid a small annual sum in acknowledgement of Foley ownership of the land. The committee had evidence of this when it was approached by an encroacher seeking advice. He had been threatened with legal action by the agent of Lady Foley, lady of the manor of Malvern, because he had encroached by adding an extension to his house. He claimed that if he signed an acknowledgement and paid a small annual sum there would be no legal proceedings. But, of course, Lady Foley and her agent had the law on their side – from 1235 until it was effectively repealed in 1893 the Statute of Merton enabled any lord of any manor to 'approve' any common surplus to the needs of the inhabitants. Lady Foley could not only use this law to her advantage but also appear generous in assisting poorer people to enjoy improved housing conditions.

Nationally, such actions by manorial lords became so widespread that the Commons Preservation Society, founded in 1865, became a key player in destroying the power of the Statute of Merton in the 1890s.* Locally, the Malvern committee had made little impact by 1870, when the editor of *The Malvern News*, rival to *The Malvern Advertiser*, did not mince his words. On 30 April he expressed his opinion as to where responsibility for the hills lay:

---

* Lord Eversley, *Commons, Forests and Footpaths*, 1910, Chap. VIII, pp. 203-13.

Is there a Manor of Malvern? and if so, who is its Lord? Does that Lord keep a steward? and where is he to be found? I ask these questions because the commons are in such a wretched condition. Talk about a dung-heap! a mixen! or any other place equally filthy and you have an idea of these. Why not keep them in proper order?... Look at the disgraceful condition of some parts; ruts here, rubbish there; broken glass lying down by tin crippings; old mortar and shavings shaking hands; while blades of grass that should be green have their faces begrimed with the shakings of some soot bag. Surely these commons might be made places of pleasant resort – promenades where people could stroll and enjoy themselves. Is there no-one in authority to look after them? ... There are notice-boards in some places – but they are dummies, and no-one cares for them ... Let a committee, self-constituted, set to work to collect subscriptions and expend them in putting in order the commons in this neighbourhood.

This undoubtedly struck a chord with his readers but, although there was widespread agreement that something must be done about the erosion and disfigurement of Malvern's commons and landscape, there was no such agreement about what, exactly, was needed.

In 1876 a Malvern Hills Preservation Committee was set up but found it impossible to solve all of the many problems referred to in *The Malvern News* of 22 November 1879:

The frequent encroachment by squatters, the defacements of the hills, by cutting turf, and other injuries to the surface, showed that much remained to be done ... to preserve the Malvern Hills in their present beauty and prevent those defacements and encroachments that were continually being made.

The Committee got so far in 1882 as drafting a bill intended as the basis of an Act of Parliament, but in so doing it deeply offended holders of traditional common rights. The Committee's proposals failed to recognise and provide adequate safeguards for the historic rights of local freeholders, tenants and commoners, who had a further cause for grievance – the bill included plans to empower a newly established body to set aside specific areas for recreation and regulate sports and games, marking out pitches and the like. Such plans would reduce the area available for grazing and give new rights to people with no historic entitlement to them.

Feelings ran very high. In November 1882 all freeholders, tenants and commoners were invited to discuss the 'advantages or disadvantages of the bill which is proposed' at a meeting in Colwall, stronghold of Stephen Ballard, stalwart defender of commons and common rights. In addition to the 'objectionable clauses' in the proposed bill, the Malvern Hills Committee, dominated by Malvern men, was perceived by some as being in the pocket of the lady of the manor, Lady Foley, and therefore reluctant to tackle her ready agreement to encroachment. Recognising that it had failed adequately to address important issues, the committee withdrew its bill and the baton was passed to a new committee led by men like Stephen Ballard and Robert Raper, an Oxford don, who persuaded his lawyer friend John Gent to draft a new bill. This new bill became the first Malvern Hills Act of 1884.

This Act should be seen in the national context. Successive governments in the 19th century were becoming less and less *laissez-faire*. A growing sense of the need for government intervention to secure a fairer society and to address environmental issues led, for example, to the Commons Act of 1876, aiming at the provision of large public recreation areas throughout the country. This was less successful than had been hoped because opposition from manorial lords or from commoners exercising their rights thwarted schemes aimed primarily at public enjoyment. In 1877 the New Forest Act safeguarded the New Forest for the future use of commoners and for the enjoyment of the public at large.[*] The idea was emerging that land could be not only used by commoners but also enjoyed by others. Events in Malvern illustrate the delicacy of balancing the very different interests of manorial lords, commoners and the public but the issues were addressed with a spirit of co-operation, enabling a remarkable compromise to be reached. The long-standing rights of specifically named manorial lords and of commoners had to be preserved. That done, the Malvern freeholders, tenants and commoners were prepared to agree to public access to their commons. The Malvern Hills Conservators, set up by the 1884 Act, were given responsibility to regulate common rights and to enforce their own bye-laws over land in Great Malvern, Mathon, Cradley, Colwall and Hanley Castle – the heart of the former Malvern Chase. Their *raison d'être* was to prevent any further erosion of the common land, for the twin purposes of preserving common rights for locals

[*] Lord Eversley, *op.cit.* p.167.

75 *Advertisement for the historic 1882 meeting which led to the foundation of the Malvern Hills Conservators.*

76 *An unusual view from the foot of the Herefordshire Beacon to the British Camp Hotel, now known as the* Malvern Hills Hotel. *Published by Woods, The Royal Library, about 1890.*

and providing recreational areas for the public at large. They were given a small budget, obtained through a precept of not more than a halfpenny in the pound out of the rates of the parishes of Great Malvern, Colwall and Mathon. Since there were 240 old pence in the pound, the sum raised was small – about £165 a year. Even *The Times*, whose interest in the matter indicated the importance being attached nationally to the Malvern Hills, thought this a tiny amount for the management of land of little agricultural value but of huge importance for public recreation. Time was to prove that it rendered the Conservators impotent to solve the serious problem of quarrying, which emerged within 20 years of the passing of the Act.

During their early days the Conservators were served by a particularly well qualified, conscientious and well educated ranger, Alexander King. A surveyor who lived in Colwall, he was a freeholder and commoner who pastured his sheep on the hills and kept a vigilant eye on the lands entrusted to his supervision from 1884 until his death in 1922. The books containing his reports give details which, like the 16th-century record of Henry Dingley, paint a vivid account of life in Malvern Chase country.

77   The café, which served climbers on the Worcestershire Beacon for about a hundred years until it burned down in the late 20th century. Breakfast here was a traditional midsummer morning feature.

Since the Conservators had to prevent erosion of common land, many instances of alleged encroachment had to be investigated. Alexander King reported on these cases, sometimes giving quite colourful detail. There was, for example, a man called Green

> living in a very unsightly hut which he has erected near the Wych. He often keeps a great quantity of pigs and all round the front of his dwelling he has erected temporary pigs cots or runs, which have increased from time to time. ...This great nuisance must be very obnoxious to visitors who have to pass near it to get from the Wych on to the Beacon.

By March 1885 Green was reported as being 'So very deaf and stupid that no-one can make him understand anything'. But was he so stupid? Six months later he and his pigs were still in residence, even though his 13 pigs were filthy, and the foulness of the wash with which they were fed 'very much endangers the health of the people who have to reside in the vicinity'.

Green and his pigs presented two quite separate but widespread problems – encroachment and public health – which the Conservators not infrequently faced in their early years. In August 1885 a woman claimed that

> she had for years made use of a hole or pit, which is situate upon the Common, near to her property, for the purpose of depositing night soil from the earth closets which are attached to the whole of her cottages – I inspected this pit and found it full, but as plenty of ashes were used no nuisance was perceptible [*sic*]

By 8 May 1885 King had produced a list of 61 encroachments which he had found in his first five months in office, but to get them thrown open he had to produce witnesses to vouch for the fact of the land having been enclosed within the last 12 years. This was not easy. On 6 November 1885 he wrote:

> There was a serious riot at the Wych last night, and from the information I gather I believe the affair was as much intended to intimidate witnesses from giving evidence in future as to spite them for past activities.

In August 1886 he had difficulty in getting witnesses concerning a right of way over an enclosure: 'Jno. Pitt was the only man who would attend without being forced and he would only attend if fetched in a carriage'. People continued to leave rubbish, including a quantity of broken glass, on the hills which 'in my opinion is a great source of danger to the feet of animals'.

Opportunities to make a shilling or two were eagerly seized by some people with land bordering on the commons. They kept 'bad fences and badly fastened gates for no other purpose than that of making a profit by impounding sheep'. One such enterprising man had demanded and received about £3 from several sheep-owners before giving them back their sheep. They were so vexed that they paid a blacksmith to make and fix a fastening to one gate. Another man, with a garden opposite the *Redan Inn* in North Malvern, having caught 18 sheep in his garden, had 'put 6d a head upon them.'

The ranger's duties were varied and he had to report anything untoward. Illegal fern-cutting, sheep-worrying and gypsies setting up camp were regularly mentioned in his reports to the Conservators for they were naturally perennial problems. More out of the ordinary was his drive one winter morning (14 January 1885)

> to the Old Elm at Barnard's Green through Hall Green and up Sherrard's Green. I thoroughly inspected the Old Elm but could find no trace of any fire having been kindled inside the tree.

This elm, on the Guarlford Road, survived until the middle of the 20th century and was also known as the friar's elm (see p. 28).

By September 1885 it was clear that the work of ranging the hills was too much for one man so two haywardens were appointed to assist Alexander King, who supervised them and continued to range the more outlying regions. One of the first things reported by Haywarden Pantin was damage done to the turf by pigs without rings through their noses – a late 19th-century reference to a problem recorded in parishes, including those in Malvern Chase, from time immemorial. In Upton in 1743, for example, unringed pigs were reported by the churchwardens as doing rather worse than damaging the turf – having climbed on to the low mound round the church they 'root among ye graves'.

About the time of Queen Victoria's golden jubilee, a controversial new road was built between the Wyche Cutting and British Camp. People with grazing rights resented the use of 10 or 12 acres of grazing land for this purpose, and feared that what they perceived as an indulgence for visitors would be the first of similar 'works of defacement round the whole circuit of the hills'. It proved difficult to finance the new road, which was completed behind schedule. Appropriately named Jubilee Drive, it proved to be unequal to the task of bearing an unexpectedly heavy amount of traffic. Ultimately, however, it became almost universally popular and, once responsibility for it was taken over by the county authorities in the 1920s, the problem of maintenance was resolved. It remains a most convenient scenic road from which beautiful views across Herefordshire may be enjoyed – spectacular at most times, but perhaps especially so as the sun is setting.

The subject of roads brings us to the single most obvious problem with which the Conservators wrestled in the first half of the 20th century – quarrying. Contrary to popular myth, the Conservators were not founded to stop quarrying. Indeed, so urgent was the need to buy off manorial lords' opposition to the setting up of the Conservators, that Clause 13 of the 1884 Act specifically guaranteed to them ancient quarrying rights:

> as now belong to them of digging and getting by open quarrying or otherwise any
> stone mines or other minerals within or under the said lands.

Unlike the Forest of Dean, with its valuable coal and iron mines, Malvern Forest had never been a source of mineral wealth. When the guarantee was made in Clause 13 no-one foresaw that Malvern stone, which fragments and so is of limited use for house building, would make, when crushed, superb foundations for the new roads which became necessary in the early 20th century. When motor cars and lorries took over from horses as a main means of transport the quality of road building had to improve, so the Conservators fought in the early years of the new century to preserve the hills from the depredations

78   *Quarry workers in the early 20th century.*

79 *A threat sent to Fred Bal-lard, chairman of the Malvern Hills Conservators, when they sought in the early 1920s to curtail the quarrying.*

of commercial quarriers who had leased from manorial lords quarrying rights so innocently guaranteed to them in 1884. A second Malvern Hills Act in 1909 was intended to address the problem of quarrying. Unfortunately all clauses relating to quarrying were removed during the parliamentary process since the Conservators lacked the financial means to compensate manorial lords for the loss of quarrying rights guaranteed to them in 1884. A third Act in 1924 empowered the Conservators to raise loans, serviced by an increased precept on local rates. This facilitated their compulsory purchase of certain manorial rights and quarries, and enabled them to preserve the skyline in key places along the ridge of the hills.

In 1925 the Conservators paid the Foley family £16,092 for the manor of Malvern, thus adding to the board's area of jurisdiction over 600 acres of prime land, including parts of central Malvern such as Belle Vue Island, Edith Walk and Back Lane. This purchase was achieved with greater goodwill than had been apparent in the early dealings between the board and the Foley interest.

There was, however, insufficient money to buy out all the quarrying rights so the struggle over quarrying reached something of a climax in the 1930s, when two groups fought over the Malverns. On the one hand were quarry companies claiming the value of keeping men in work during a period of high unemployment, and on the other hand were those conscious of the hills' vulner-ability and desperate to preserve their natural beauty. Photographs taken in the first half of the 20th century illustrate the damage done to the hills, much of it visible from some distance away. Closer to hand the noise and dangers of quarrying operations shattered the tranquillity traditionally associated with the Malverns.

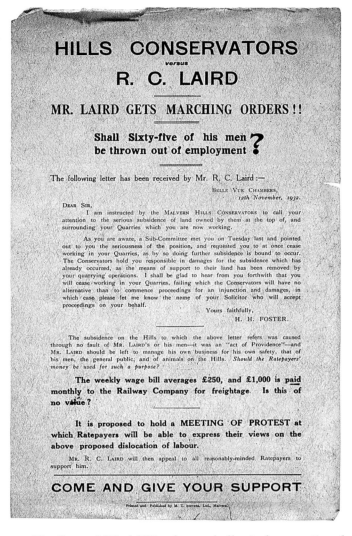

HILLS CONSERVATORS
versus
R. C. LAIRD

MR. LAIRD GETS MARCHING ORDERS !!

Shall Sixty-five of his men be thrown out of employment ?

The following letter has been received by Mr. R. C. Laird:—

BELLE VUE CHAMBERS,
12th November, 1932.

DEAR SIR,

I am instructed by the MALVERN HILLS CONSERVATORS to call your attention to the serious subsidence of land owned by them at the top of, and surrounding your Quarries which you are now working.

As you are aware, a Sub-Committee met you on Tuesday last and pointed out to you the seriousness of the position, and requested you to at once cease working in your Quarries, as by so doing further subsidence is bound to occur. The Conservators hold you responsible in damages for the subsidence which has already occurred, as the means of support to their land has been removed by your quarrying operations. I shall be glad to hear from you forthwith that you will cease working in your Quarries, failing which the Conservators will have no alternative than to commence proceedings for an injunction and damages, in which case please let me know the name of your Solicitor who will accept proceedings on your behalf.

Yours faithfully,
H. H. FOSTER.

The subsidence on the Hills to which the above letter refers was caused through no fault of MR. LAIRD's or his men—it was an "act of Providence"—and MR. LAIRD should be left to manage his own business for his own safety, that of his men, the general public, and of animals on the Hills. *Should the Ratepayers' money be used for such a purpose?*

The weekly wage bill averages £250, and £1,000 is paid monthly to the Railway Company for freightage. Is this of no value?

It is proposed to hold a MEETING OF PROTEST at which Ratepayers will be able to express their views on the above proposed dislocation of labour.

MR. R. C. LAIRD will then appeal to all reasonably-minded Ratepayers to support him.

COME AND GIVE YOUR SUPPORT

Printed and Published by M. T. Stevens, Ltd., Malvern.

80 *This leaflet, published by quarriers when the Malvern Hills Conservators sought to prevent their inflicting further damage on the hills, sums up the mid-1930s controversy. Quarrying provided jobs, but the amounts that Mr Laird indignantly pointed out he was paying in wages and freight charges actually made his opponents' point – his quarrying was causing significant damage to the hills.*

The Second World War focused all minds on national survival, incidentally, as wars so often do, ending the unemployment crisis. Desperate times required desperate measures, and during the war, when Britain needed to be as self-sufficient as possible, 54 acres of Castlemorton Common were ploughed and planted with potatoes and oats to help with food supplies. After the war it returned to open common land, which it remains to this day, now under the jurisdiction of the Malvern Hills Conservators to whom, in the 1960s, the Church Commissioners, as lords of the manor, made over nearly 700 acres for a nominal sum of £2,115.

After the Second World War, too, the apparently insurmountable problem of quarrying was at last amicably resolved and, as we shall see, much of the former Malvern Chase was to achieve a new status.[*]

---

[*] Further details on the establishment and early work of the Malvern Hills Conservators may be found in Pamela Hurle, *The Malvern Hills, A Hundred Years of Conservation,* 1984.

XIV

Post-war Consolidation and Malvern Chase Today

Legislation in the 1940s and 1950s showed post-war governments recognising their responsibility to protect that which, once destroyed, is lost for ever. In 1949 the National Parks and Access to the Countryside Act marked a recognition of the dangers of increased urbanisation of our society and the consequent threat to some of the most beautiful landscapes in England and Wales. The Act sought to protect, for the enjoyment of future generations, areas that the Countryside Agency (re-named Natural England in November 2006) and other bodies describe as an irreplaceable part of our national heritage. Under the terms of the Act, over 50 areas have been designated National Parks or Areas of Outstanding Natural Beauty, the Malvern Hills being included in a relatively small AONB of 40 square miles so designated in 1959. The hills themselves form about a tenth – but the most vital tenth, dominating the surrounding countryside – of the somewhat pear-shaped Malvern Hills Area of Outstanding Natural Beauty, which stretches from Knightwick in the north to Bromsberrow in the south, and from Ledbury and Wellington Heath in the west to Welland in the east. Whilst National Parks actively encourage public enjoyment of the countryside, the Areas of Outstanding Natural Beauty have for many years now seen their main task as conservation. Any designated Area may encompass land used for a variety of purposes, and designation does not imply ownership. Within the Malvern Hills Area of Outstanding Natural Beauty are 3,000 acres under the jurisdiction of the Malvern Hills Conservators. The officers of both organisations work in sympathy with each other's aims – indeed Malvern Hills Conservators provide accommodation for AONB officers in the building purchased by the Conservators in 1995 – but there is a clear distinction between their roles.

During the 30 years after the Second World War, despite their new AONB status and the long-standing concern of the Malvern Hills Conservators, parts of the Malvern Hills were still being quarried. But coincidentally with the protection afforded by AONB status, other factors made quarrying less attractive to the quarriers themselves. Some quarries, worked down to, or almost to, the water table, were at the point of becoming uneconomic, as pumping out water was costly. Road-building schemes and techniques were changing, and central government was intervening much more in road-building plans as well as in environmental issues. An inquiry by the Minister of Housing and Local Government in the early 1950s led to a ministerial decision in 1953 that ultimately all quarrying on the Malverns should cease, though the process would be gradual so as to avoid adverse effects on the economy and employment. All quarrying ceased on the

81   *Gullet quarry in the 1980s.*

hills when the Gullet quarry closed in 1977. As the quarriers moved out, the Malvern Hills Conservators embarked on programmes of rehabilitation which gave some of the quarry-scarred areas a rugged beauty, quite different from their original natural state, but nevertheless remarkably attractive. At Earnslaw, for example, the closure of the quarry in the 1960s enabled the provision of a much needed car-park close to the heart of the former quarry, which was transformed: filled with natural spring water in which perch and rudd were put and bred successfully, it changed from a noisy, ugly eye-sore to an attractive retreat, now further enhanced by an easy access trail to the lake. At North Hill the quarry faces were planted with grass and trees, while at the southern end of the range, where quarrying continued until the 1970s, the Conservators marked their centenary in 1984 by quite spectacular landscaping at the former Gullet quarry.

The Church Commissioners had long been impressed by the efforts of the Malvern Hills Conservators. In the early 1960s, it was their conveyance of nearly 700 acres of their land at Castlemorton Common to the Conservators which increased the area of jurisdiction of that body to a total of about 3,000 acres of the former chase, safeguarded for the benefit of both tourists and commoners. In 1923, the Rev. and Mrs H. Somers-Cocks had given land at Midsummer Hill, at the southern end of the Malverns, to the National Trust, in memory of their son killed in the First World War. So, between these two bodies and designated as an Area of Outstanding Natural Beauty, the region now has considerable protection after having been seriously threatened in less enlightened times. Nevertheless, as we shall eventually see, the pressures of commerce are strong and persistent, most privately owned land being unprotected by safeguards enshrined in the constitutions of owning bodies such as the Conservators and the National Trust.

There seem always to have been myth and misunderstanding about common land but the 1950s and 1960s saw this national confusion exacerbated when land requisitioned by the wartime government was to be returned to its previous owners and commoners. Common land might be a large expanse of grassland, a few yards of roadside verge, a village green or even the local rubbish dump. Those who claimed ownership also came in various guises, from locals using it for grazing to passing motorists stopping for a picnic. Nationally it became necessary to decide what land had to be returned to whom, while in the Malvern area it became necessary to ascertain just who was entitled to common rights and precisely what those rights were. It is perhaps surprising that the Conservators had not addressed these questions in the 80 years of their existence, but they had been preoccupied with pressing problems of encroachment and quarrying – and criticised for legal bills thus incurred. The issue of exercising common rights was not a pressing one and, since they were naturally cautious about incurring legal costs, they presumably saw no point in raising issues which had presented no particular problem.

But in 1956 the Conservators received unprecedented numbers of letters containing the same dreaded word – sheep. The animals had got out of hand, invading gardens, often jumping fences and breaking down hedges, to devour flowers and vegetables. Determined to wander, they displayed stubbornness and habits which were a particular shock to those unfamiliar with country living, as they fouled pavements and shops, bleated day and night and even jumped off walls into the path of fast moving vehicles, causing accidents. In 1956 more than 50 sheep were killed by traffic. Many correspondents wanted their owners prosecuted, seeing them as cruelly leaving animals unattended on common land which yielded so little fodder that the creatures were driven by hunger to seek food in the most unlikely places, including shops in the middle of Malvern.

The Conservators compiled a register of all who claimed common rights. Thirty-seven claimants thought they had the right to put animals on the commons around Malvern. Some believed they might graze any number, others specified perhaps 50 sheep or 20 cattle. One claimed he could graze as many sheep, cattle, horses, goats, geese and fowls as he liked wherever he liked on the commons, while several made vague claims about grazing all kinds of stock at any time of year. The grounds on which the claims were made were equally diverse and, in the claimants' total ignorance of common law, curiously optimistic. Several thought that owning land adjacent to common land conferred rights, and one man based his claim on military service in the Second World War supported by having grazed sheep on the hills for 20 years. Many thought that enjoying such a long-standing custom for a number of years established common rights, the magic number of years required to qualify varying from ten to about thirty. A few claimants referred to deeds vaguely citing the laws of Malvern Chase.

While this was happening in Malvern, a Royal Commission on Common Land led to the 1965 Commons Registration Act. The Conservators' clerk, Colonel E.D.L. Whatley, and his secretary produced a list of those genuinely entitled to common rights and then a stint was worked out. This allowed successful claimants to put on the commons a number of animals proportionate to the land they owned. All animals had to be clearly marked, the Conservators holding a list of owners and their marks so that owners of animals causing, or experiencing, trouble became for the first time easily traceable. The Conservators have always been keen, not only to protect grazing, but actively to encourage it because sheep are able easily to get into places not readily accessible to machinery, thus keeping down gorse and bracken. Reducing scrub, small trees and bracken is vital because, if allowed to spread unchecked, they can be a fire hazard and also threaten vulnerable species such as the rare high brown fritillary butterfly. The ancient hill forts on Midsummer Hill (National Trust land) and the Herefordshire Beacon are, like the shire ditch, scheduled as Ancient Monuments, and effective management of the scrubland is necessary also to protect them – both above and below ground level – to safeguard archaeological evidence.

Unfortunately, after all the work to sort out commoners' rights, there has been, in the last 30 or 40 years, a further development. Although in 2006 it is encouraging to see cattle as well as sheep on the hills and commons, there is a decline in grazing compared with its past levels. In November 2005 about 300 commoners were registered with rights to graze, but only seven actually had animals grazing on the considerable expanse of Castlemorton Common. The decline in grazing was brought about by several factors: risks to animals, especially sheep, from traffic, uncontrolled dogs and even theft have made farmers less enthusiastic about leaving them on the commons. The result has been a problem for the Conservators as scrub and trees spread over land once kept free from them by grazing animals. The ancient bare hills which gave Malvern its name are being covered with vegetation which restricts access, as well as changing the appearance and nature of the terrain and posing fire hazards. It is also now recognised that more vulnerable species of wildlife are very seriously threatened by excessive growth of more robust species. There is also the long-standing dilemma of reconciling the diverse interests of the various users of the common, as well as the interests of the land itself. Those who care for the Areas of Outstanding Natural Beauty are conscious, as the Malvern Hills Conservators have been since the 19th century, of the delicate – and changing – balance of numerous interests. Extensive consultation and the establishment of a Joint Advisory Committee in the 1990s represent official attempts to co-ordinate the protection of diverse interests in the Area of Outstanding Natural Beauty. It is hoped that such efforts bring greater understanding. Already local inhabitants are showing greater support for grazing as they perceive its benefits.

Protecting the interests of two somewhat opposing camps – of commoners and walkers – has proved to be something of a balancing act for the Conservators ever since their foundation in 1884. Grazing rights and public access can present a serious test of peaceful co-existence. Things came to a head in 1974, when the difficulties of reconciling such different interests were vividly illustrated.[*] During the lambing season a local farmer shot, in separate incidents, three dogs which he believed were worrying or about to worry his ewes grazing on the hills. Enraged that their pets might be at risk from a trigger-happy farmer, people complained to the local press and the Conservators. Others were alarmed at the potential risk to innocent bystanders, and the tourist industry feared that the publicity might frighten off visitors, with or without their dogs, which naturally display varying degrees of obedience. Whilst the farmer's action undoubtedly caused genuine distress and shock, both he and the Conservators, on whose land the shooting

---

* Pamela Hurle, *The Malvern Hills, A Hundred Years of Conservation*, 1984, p.108 and reports in *The Malvern Gazette* in the spring of 1974.

82 *The Conservators' flock.*

took place, had valid reasons for what had occurred. Even those opposed to
the use of a gun in any circumstances usually recognise the dilemma lying in
the fact that a dead or dying sheep that has been attacked by a dog can be an
even more unpleasant sight than that of a shot dog. Such hazards for stock are
an obvious disincentive to putting animals to graze on the commons. There are
less obvious, but even more fundamental, reasons for the sharp decline in the
ancient practice. Since the war, and especially in the last 20 years, farming has
been in decline, an unforeseen development causing change in the landscape that
in medieval times was afforested.

In the 1970s and 1980s grazing ponies became quite a feature, often tethered
on the grass verges of land under the Conservators' jurisdiction. There are now
few of them, presumably because owners have found, like farmers, that the
risks of theft or injury are too high. There are also animal welfare considera-
tions, tethered ponies attracting particular sympathy in extremes of hot or cold
weather. The increase in vegetation resulting from the decline in grazing caused
the Conservators to experiment by introducing their own flocks of sheep and
employing shepherds – and a dog.

Controlled burning has also taken place, sometimes to the consternation
of local residents. Any method of systematic clearance of gorse and bracken
seems to offend as many people as it pleases. Such controversy spreads into
other aspects of management of this Area of Outstanding Natural Beauty of
which, as we have seen, the Conservators have jurisdiction over only part. Lack
of economic interest in the hills and commons for grazing seems also to have
shifted the balance of interests to favour tourism. Traditionalists and locals are
somewhat uneasy that the use of the hills and commons may become primarily
as a playground, geared to the wishes and convenience of tourists.

83   *A small corner of Castlemorton Common during the travellers' invasion.*

   Money, of course, is also a factor. The Conservators still derive nearly a third of their income from the precept first raised in the 1880s from local council tax payers. Now called a levy, it currently brings in about £320,000 a year. Many visitors contribute nothing whatever to the costs incurred in caring for the hills and commons, some priding themselves on avoiding parking fees for the vehicles which bring them from distant places. For them the hills offer a virtually free day out and some locals, paying an average levy of about £25 per household a year, feel a degree of antipathy to helping to finance this. Fortunately the Conservators have increasingly managed to secure grants from national bodies such as English Nature, the Countryside Agency and the Heritage Lottery Fund to finance specific projects. Rehabilitation of some of the areas damaged by quarrying, the landscaping of landmarks on the hills and the provision of cattle grids to stop grazing animals wandering are all examples of projects paid for by such grants. Car parking fees, perceived as a fair means of attempting to make those who enjoy the hills contribute to the costs, bring in about £150,000 a year.
   Whilst the medieval chase offered the pleasures of hunting to a privileged few, that same area today provides a playground for all kinds of visitors. Walkers are the most numerous, but ball-games, kite flying, hang-gliding, horse-riding and other activities all have their enthusiasts. All of them – over a million a year, with no respite even in the winter – take a huge toll on the natural beauty of the Malverns. Medieval farmers, hampered by the protection given to depredating deer by forest law, struggled against nature to wrest a living from the soil, failing too often to produce enough to feed all the hungry mouths dependent on their labour. If a medieval peasant might somehow be projected into the 21st century, he would probably be surprised to find that today we have become conscious of how vulnerable nature itself can be. Year on year, millions of feet wear out the soil covering the hills and commons, threatening also the delicate flora and fauna which once flourished. Many people benefit in many ways from tourism but an unpleasant reality at last being recognised is that the tourist is always in danger of destroying by his very presence the phenomenon he has come to enjoy. Especially if he comes in convoy with several thousand others. Castlemorton briefly hit the national headlines in 1992, when an estimated 20,000 new-age travellers decided to camp on its common for some days, causing distress with their most

unwelcome noise and the rubbish they left behind for local people to clear away over the succeeding days and weeks. Destruction of wildlife also occurred, though precisely how much it is difficult to assess.

Notwithstanding damage done by visitors, there are still places where one can see small leaved lime trees, wild service trees, dormice or nightingales – all descendants of those here hundreds of years ago. The publicity literature and the management guidelines published by the staff of the Area of Outstanding Natural Beauty are full of interesting information too detailed to include here, but vital reading for those concerned with the future of the region. It analyses the nature of various soil types and gives details of land use, pointing out that 20 per cent of the AONB is covered by trees, though the Malvern Hills themselves are not so heavily wooded. This is twice the national average, and includes an extraordinarily wide variety of both deciduous and evergreen species. Furthermore, over half of this is classified as Ancient Semi-Natural Woodland continuously wooded for at least 400 years and often very much longer. That takes us back to the time when forest law operated, and is very significant in the preservation of wildlife over countless generations. It follows from this that the Malverns shelter rare species of wildlife, and contain several designated Sites of Special Scientific Interest (SSSI) and Special Wildlife Sites (SWS). Rather like medieval forest law which sought to protect the venison and the vert, modern management protects vulnerable and rather less obvious species. Management of an area which includes a wide variety of landscapes must take into consideration the need to protect these sites as well as addressing practical and economic realities.

84   *Harebells.*

85   *Primroses.*

86   *Waxcaps.*

87   *Earth star.*

88   *Wood anemones.*

89   *Winter berries.*

Coppicing and pollarding – cutting out the top growth from trees – are traditional practices which since time immemorial have prolonged the life of trees and provided the natural habitat of many species of birds, insects and other animals. The growth thus removed from trees might provide material for fencing, charcoal and other uses. On Castlemorton Common there are some very old and rare pollarded black poplars which are prime specimens of this type of woodland management. Very old trees may have been significant landmarks, the valley of 'the white leaved oak', for example, featuring in Henry Dingley's 1584 perambulation.

The 1949 ideal of protecting scenic beauty has thus been broadened in the last half century, a process which has intensified in the last 20 years. The Countryside Act of 1968 and the Environment Act of 1995 emphasised the need to protect geological and cultural features as well as wildlife. Whilst pedestrian right of access ('the right to roam') has added to the responsibilities of bodies within the Areas of Outstanding Natural Beauty, the Malvern Hills Conservators have long experience of public rights of access to the hills and commons on foot and on horseback. The cynical might feel, as in so many fields where government has sought to regulate, that practicalities have sometimes been lost in the welter of paperwork and meetings, but there is no doubting the dedication and competence of those who look after the Malvern Hills. Furthermore, it has never been so easy to find out what these bodies are doing, since their reports, their professional publications and their web-sites provide a mass of high-quality information.

The Conservators have sometimes been criticised, especially by those who are neither knowledgeable nor willing

90 *Cattle grazing by pollarded poplars on Castlemorton Common in 2000. There are nearly 100 pollarded black poplars on land under the jurisdiction of the Malvern Hills Conservators, who are trying to prolong their life by pollarding and to preserve the species by propagation.*

91 *The old millpond at Castlemorton, providing a home for waterfowl.*

to understand the delicate balance of interests they must consider, but it would be difficult to find a body with so long and so commendable a record of achievement. Of the 29 Conservators, 11 are directly chosen by the local electorate, and 18 are nominated by the Church Commissioners (1), Malvern Hills District Council (8), Worcestershire County Council (5), Herefordshire Council (2) and by Colwall (1), and Mathon (1) Parish Councils. Although such nominations may reflect the political party colour of the majority in the councils, party politics have never been a significant feature in the Conservators' deliberations. This absence of party politics may well be an important contribution to the success of the board. Another important feature is the financial autonomy of the board. Individual Conservators receive no payment for their work though, of course, their employees on the ground and in the office are paid. The most substantial outgoings are on conservation work on the 3,000 acres controlled by the board. As their then clerk, Col. E.D.L. Whatley, noted in the 1970s:

> The Conservators feel that their history and successful efforts at conservation ... make a very strong case for national parks and areas like the Malvern Hills being managed by an autonomous body whose sole concern is the conservation of the area. If the administration is carried out by a Committee or a County authority it has to take its place with other committees. Because of the nature of the work of conservation other matters seemingly more pressing may tend to squeeze out the conservation and the countryside committee may become the poor relation. ...The Conservators think that it is essential that if the administration body is to be independent it should have control of its own finances, i.e. a right to precept, which should be limited. The alternative is an annual negotiation for funds from either the Government or local authority who would really be able to control the conservancy power through the purse strings.

92   *Motorists need to be prepared for unexpected encounters on Castlemorton Common.*

93 *Malvern Hills Conservators field staff replacing a seat on the hills.*

94 *After clearing some of the scrub it is carefully burned. Malvern Hills Conservators field staff work throughout the year to ensure that the hills and commons are well maintained. Their role is central to the principles of conservation: the modern myth that nature is best served if man does nothing at all is now, happily, being questioned. Our great 'natural' forests bear the imprint of man's management over the centuries: without that intervention they would have deteriorated, as ancient trees outgrew their strength, younger vegetation gave up the struggle to grow through a mass of undergrowth and some species became extinct through being smothered.*

95 *Controlled burning by field staff is vital in managing scrub on the hills. Accidental fires are a serious hazard.*

For over a hundred years the Conservators appointed a lawyer as their clerk, a post phased out in the 1990s. The last lawyer clerk was David Judge who saw through the passing of the fifth Malvern Hills Act in 1995. The internal administration has now changed, placing more emphasis on visitor management as well as conservation. The current Director is Ian Rowat, with experience in countryside management, a profession recognised only in the last 40 years. But key features remain. One of these is the use of a committee structure to ensure that, before any important decision is made by the full board, extensive research and discussion tease out all the relevant facts so that decisions are informed. Some may not be unanimous, and the Conservators have occasionally been criticised rather publicly by some of their own members. The Conservators and their staff are generally held locally in high regard by those who have taken the trouble to find out the facts. Money and resources are carefully husbanded: a small office staff and a skilled field staff of six led by an operations manager represents very good value for the local taxpayers' money. The work of three paid wardens is also supplemented by six volunteer wardens.

In addition to the obvious attractions of the hills and commons, the former Malvern Chase still contains farms and orchards which specialise in 'pick your own' fruit, some of it being varieties not available in the supermarkets and other large stores. Soft fruits such as strawberries, raspberries, gooseberries and blackcurrants are popular, as are tree fruits such as apples and pears that are still grown locally and can be bought in local shops. The damson tree was for long a common species in hedgerows, the fruit possibly providing dye as well as food. Grassland underlying the fruit trees often shelters a wide variety of flora and fauna.

Sadly, both dairy and sheep farming have significantly declined in recent years, disease, economic pressures and government policies all contributing to a sense of despair amongst those who still, like the medieval inhabitants of the chase, seek their living from the soil. The impact of supermarkets is a controversial issue, much of the nation's food now being flown in from around the world. Land that once supported livestock and arable crops to feed the population now carries little of either, and the nature of the landscape is changing. Farmers are now paid to manage land rather than grow food. Those still producing food often have tender crops under polythene tunnels or – particularly in Herefordshire – are accused of destroying archaeological features by ploughing for extensive potato production. These are but two of the controversial practices of this region, making life very different from how it was even one generation ago. Similarly, the battle between those who see the countryside as a playground or a beautiful idyll and those who live and work in it is emotionally charged. Some may even see in it some kind of modern equivalent of the older struggle between distant authorities who made the forest laws and those who had to live with the effects of such legislation. Urbanites become – rightly or wrongly – suspected of romantic illusions about nature or a desire to plant refreshment stalls and lavatories while local residents become – rightly or wrongly – suspected of wanting selfishly to keep a national treasure for their private profit or enjoyment.

Great Malvern town centre – built on a steep slope – has long presented a challenge to retailers. Their difficulties in attracting trade were compounded when in the 1990s the local council encouraged commercial activity on flat land

96 *A good example of the ancient craft of hedge-laying which produces a stock-proof barrier.*

at the town's most northerly boundary, where Malvern Link meets Newland. Ill-feeling accompanied the building of the resultant new roads from Malvern Link towards the east in order to open up a retail park and science park. Many Malvern inhabitants nurture a fierce determination to protect the visual impact as perceived from the hills and to resist any more large-scale development. This is not simply the self-serving phenomenon of the nimby proclaiming 'not in my backyard' and seeking to protect house values. It stems from a concern about environmental values and a desire to protect the area from creeping development – driven by fears perhaps rather similar to those expressed in the 19th century by the men who sought to stop the erosion of common land.

Developers, of course, have a different perception. Within the area of the old chase some villages, such as Welland, have seen building development but not on the very large scale of a new town. Upton has its housing estates and Malvern has expanded to an even greater extent, especially with the 19th-century water-cure, the growth of the education industry and the arrival of scientists in 1942 to work on devices which were to be vital in the victory over Hitler. Initial hostility to them seems not to have been due to fears that they would create a long-term need for new houses, since much of Malvern fervently hoped and believed that they would go away as soon as the war ended, giving little thought to future housing estates. The unfriendly reception the scientists received was much more likely to have been due to their bringing the realities of war too close for comfort – if the Germans had got wind of the work going on here Malvern would have become a prime target for enemy bombs. It transpired that the economic effect of this group of workers on Malvern was to be dramatic and lasting, comparable with and arguably very much greater than that of the water-cure which had started exactly a hundred years earlier. They stayed after the

97   Conservators field staff working during very frosty weather.

98 *Conservators field staff working in the snow.*

war, the young, usually single, scientists maturing into family men and women demanding comfortable homes, social life, cultural opportunities and good schools. One new secondary school took its name – The Chase – from the use to which the area was put in medieval times. The Malvern region was transformed by demands for all kinds of services from people educated and articulate enough to get what they wanted. The scientific establishment became the town's largest employer and created a need for extensive housing development in Malvern and the surrounding villages. The wide and varied interests of such newcomers to Malvern pumped new blood into old societies and led to the foundation of new ones. Thus, for a town of its size (30,000 to 40,000, depending on where the boundaries are drawn between Malvern and its surrounding villages) Malvern is remarkably well endowed with literary, dramatic and musical activities, adult education and a newly refurbished theatre capable of staging major productions many of which are performed here before going to London's west end.

In contrast to the development and sprawl of Malvern, the small villages have lost many of their facilities, though most still value their parish church and village pub. Village shops and post offices are under threat but a large village such as Colwall – which also has a railway station – enjoys high standards and shopping opportunities much envied by those who have lost their village baker, butcher, post office or general store.

Upton, which forty years ago looked somewhat run down, is now a flourishing little town again, though it lost its historic market more than a generation ago. Its marina on the River Severn, the age-old basis of Upton's commercial success, serves the modern business of providing a leisure facility and bringing tourists to Upton. This purpose has also been served by Upton's introduction of

99   *An autumn view towards the hills.*

events such as its very popular annual jazz festival, bringing in large numbers of people from a wide area.

Another popular venue in the heart of the former chase is the showground on which the Three Counties Agricultural Society has held its show annually since 1958. Until then, agricultural shows were held in turn in each of the three counties of Gloucestershire, Herefordshire and Worcestershire – resulting in some not very convenient sites being used. The purchase of a permanent site extending to nearly 150 acres enabled proper facilities to be set up. It also provided a superb venue for other events for which the Agricultural Society can charge rents with which they can finance continual improvements. This site, in Worcestershire but only one mile from the Herefordshire border and three from the Gloucestershire border, was described by John Hornyold in the 16th century as the 'verie harte of Malverne Chace'. It is now the heart of the three counties, and served by good roads, based on those newly set out by Hanley Castle's Enclosure Act in the 1790s. It draws hundreds of thousands of people every year to a wide variety of events such as auctions, a nationally recognised Spring Garden Show, dog shows and caravan rallies, as well as the agricultural shows for which it was originally purchased. The former playground of kings and nobles has become the playground of the masses.

100 *Despite the advance of tourism, the Malverns can still be lonely and mysterious.*

The old administrative centre of Malvern Chase – Hanley Castle – still has the school which dates back to medieval times. It now provides state secondary education for girls (first admitted in 1972) and boys from many of the surrounding parishes, outlasting a modern school built on the outskirts of Upton in 1958 and closed 30 years later. This is a remarkable achievement for a school which has passed through many crises, including the threat of closure less than 40 years ago. It bears the hallmark of a survivor – the ability to adapt to change, whilst maintaining good standards. Its buildings range from medieval through to modern times, one being the probable home of the Henry Dingley who so enjoyed his forest perambulation in 1584 that he left his record of it, giving us a glimpse of another age and world.

Many local inhabitants are conscious of both their good fortune in living in such a beautiful environment and the history surrounding it. The thinking of the last half century has shown an awareness of today's responsibilities to future generations but there is still anxiety that the pressures for development may cause irreparable damage to a vulnerable landscape.

And the deer? They may still be seen at Eastnor.

Glossary

afforestation: changing the legal status of an area by imposing forest laws to protect the 'venison and the vert' (see below) so that hunting may be exclusively enjoyed by the monarch or privileged subjects.

assarts: areas within a forest or chase cleared or developed with permission of the monarch or the lord of the chase.

attachments: fines for offences committed in the forest.

barton: a farmyard, especially one belonging to a lord of a manor.

chase: an afforested area in which hunting rights have been granted by the monarch to a favoured subject. In common parlance, the term is sometimes retained in areas where the hunting rights have been restored to the monarch.

common: arable fields or pasture land shared by numerous landowners, known as commoners, within a specific parish.

copyhold: a form of property tenure in which the tenant's entitlement was written in manorial court rolls and s/he was given a copy as proof of entitlement.

common rights: the entitlement to use common land (see above) for a variety of purposes such as grazing animals or picking up windfall wood for fuel etc.

court baron and court leet: manorial courts held usually twice a year for administration of the manor, its property and services (court baron) and for punishment of petty offences (court leet).

disafforestation: the removal of an area from the special forest laws designed to protect the 'venison and the vert' (see below).

enclosure: division of common fields, pastures or wastelands into allotments for private occupation. Enclosure Acts passed in the 18th and 19th centuries significantly reduced the acreage of open common land at that time.

encroachment: illegal absorption of common land into private occupation.

estovers: windfall branches which those exercising common rights were entitled to pick up for use as fuel or to repair their houses, tools and equipment.

forester: an official appointed to implement forest laws.

hayward or haywarden: an official appointed to supervise the management of hedges, common land and animals grazing on common land.

hombling of dogs: in order to minimise injury to protected animals such as deer, some of the claws of dogs kept in afforested areas were removed in the hombling or humbling process.

inquisitiones post mortem: written reports of enquiries into the property of a deceased person.

intercommoning: the sharing of common rights by more than one parish within a specified area. Common of vicinage is the more formal term.

keeper: an official appointed to help implement forest laws.

league: a variable length, usually about three miles, but possibly as little as half that distance.

pannage: the right to put pigs in an afforested area in order that they may benefit from eating the acorns or mast produced by the oak and beech trees.

parker: an official appointed to supervise a park (enclosed area) and the game which were protected in it.

pinfold: alternative name for the pound, used for confining stray animals.

pontage: toll imposed for crossing a bridge.

recusant: one who refused to renounce his or her Roman Catholic religion, continuing to practise it, if necessary in secret.

rider: a forest official appointed to help in the implementation of forest law.

stint: rationing the number of animals which each commoner might graze on a specified area of common land.

toll booth: a place from which a medieval market was supervised, providing a means whereby anyone with a grievance could receive a hearing.

wasteland: land, usually of too poor a quality to be used as arable, but used for a variety of purposes by those enjoying common rights. Loosely translated as common land.

venison and vert: the deer and their habitat, protected by forest law.

verderer: an official appointed to help implement forest laws.

villein: a medieval peasant, tied to the land and not free to move, marry etc without his lord's consent.

virgate: usually about 30 acres, being a quarter of a hide, which was anything between 60 and 180 acres. Medieval land measurement was reckoned by how much could be ploughed by one team in a year, so the acreage depended on the nature of the ground.

Bibliography

Primary Sources in Worcestershire Record Office
(abbreviated to WRO in footnotes)
Documents relating to Malvern Chase (some now stored at Gloucestershire Record Office).
The Berington Collection, especially documents (footnoted in text) on Malvern Chase and Little Malvern
Churchwardens' Presentments
Parish and Parochial Church Council Deposits, especially Vestry books
Tithe and enclosure awards
The Buckle Collection of drawings

Malvern Hills Conservators records
Photographic archive
Rangers' report books
Annual reports
Web site: www.malvernhills.org.uk

Manuscript Maps
1628 Map of Malvern Chase in the custody of the Society of Antiquaries, Piccadilly, London.
1633 Map of Malvern Chase in the Berington Collection in Worcestershire Record Office
1744 Maps of the manor of Malvern owned by Malvern Hills Conservators and deposited in Worcestershire Record Office

Printed Maps
1772 map of Worcestershire by Isaac Taylor
1822 map of Worcestershire by Christopher Greenwood

Unpublished Sources
Ada Ballard, Private diaries and accounts
Cora Weaver, 'Forest Law, Custom and Enclosure of Malvern Chase 1776-1884', Master of Studies in English Local History. Dissertation for Kellogg College Oxford, 1995
The Victoria County History. Notes made by the researchers in the early 20th century and deposited in Worcestershire Record Office

Published Sources

Allies, Jabez, *British, Roman and Saxon Antiquities and Folklore of Worcestershire*, Smith, 1856

Area Of Outstanding Natural Beauty, Publicity material, including web site: www.malvernhillsaonb.org.uk

Atkin, Malcolm, *The Civil War in Worcestershire*, Alan Sutton, 1995

Barnard, E.A.B., *A survey of Malvern Chase in 1628, Transactions of* Worcestershire Archaeological Society, 1929

Bethell, Hal, *Alarums and Excursions, A History of Beacons and Bonfires on the Malvern Hills*, First Paige, Malvern, 1988

Birkett, Percival, *Malvern Hills Historical Sketch compiled from Public Records and County Histories with observations*, 1882

Bowden, Mark, *The Malvern Hills, An ancient landscape*, English Heritage, 2005

Brassington, W. Salt, *Historic Worcestershire*, Midland Educational Co.1894

Bright, Allen H., *New Light on Piers Plowman*, Oxford University Press, 1928

Bryer, Ronald, *Not the Least. The Story of Little Malvern*, Self Publishing Association, 1993

Camden, William, *Britannia*, edited by Richard Gough, London, 1789

Chambers, John, *A General History of Malvern*, 1817

Cox, D.C., *This Foolish Business, Dr Nash and the Worcestershire Collections*, Worcestershire Historical Society, 1993

Davis, H.W.C., *England under the Normans and Angevins*, Methuen, 1921

Dyer, Christopher, *Bromsgrove: A small town in Worcestershire in the Middle Ages*, Worcestershire Historical Society, 2000

Earp, J.R. and Hains, B.A., *The Welsh Borderland, British Regional Geology*, H.M.S.O., 1971

Ekwall, Eilert, *The Concise Oxford Dictionary of English Place-names*, Oxford, 1990

Eversley, Lord, *Commons, Forests and Footpaths*, Cassell, 1910

Fiennes, Celia, *The Journeys of Celia Fiennes*, ed. Christopher Morris, Cresset Press 1947

Finn, R. Welldon, *Domesday Book, A Guide*, Phillimore, 1973

Gaut, R.C., *A History of Worcestershire Agriculture and Rural Evolution*, Littlebury, 1939

Habington, Thomas, *Survey of Worcestershire*, ed. John Amphlett, Worcestershire Historical Society, 1895

Hilton, R.H., *Swanimote Rolls of Feckenham Forest*, in *Miscellany I*, Worcestershire Historical Society 1960

H.M.S.O., *Malvern Hills Acts* of 1884, 1909, 1924, 1930, 1995

Hooke, Della, *Worcestershire Anglo-Saxon Charter-Bounds*, Boydell Press, 1990

Howard, J.J. and Hughes, Seymour, H., *Genealogical Collections Illustrating the History of Roman Catholic Families of England, Part IV, Hornyold*. The Wardour Press, 1892

Hurle, Pamela, *Beneath the Malvern Hills*, Hurle, 1973

Hurle, Pamela, *Hanley Castle, Heart of Malvern Chase*, Phillimore, 1977

Hurle, Pamela, *The Malvern Hills, A Hundred Years of Conservation*, Phillimore, 1984

Hurle, Pamela, *Castlemorton Farmer, John Rayer Lane 1798-1871*, Hurle, 1996

Hurle, Pamela, *Malvern Churches*, Hurle, 2002

Hurle, Pamela and Winsor, John, *Portrait of Malvern*, Phillimore, 1985

Jones, A.E.E., *Anglo-Saxon Worcester*, Ebenezer Baylis, 1958

Langland, William, *The Vision of William concerning Piers the Plowman*, edited by Rev. Walter W. Skeat, Oxford, 1968

Lawson, Emily, *Records and Traditions of Upton-upon Severn*, Houghton and Gunn, 1869

Lawson, Emily, *The Nation in the Parish*, Houghton and Gunn, 1884

Lees, Edwin, *Pictures of Nature in the Silurian Region around the Malvern Hills*, Lamb, 1856

Lees, Edwin, *The Forest and Chace of Malvern, Transactions of Malvern Naturalists' Field Club*, 1877

Lines, H.H., *The Ancient Camps on the Malvern Hills*, Philips and Probert, c.1910

Mawer, A. and Stenton, F.M., *The Place-Names of Worcestershire*, C.U.P., 1969

Minshull, G.N., *The West Midlands, A Regional Geography of the British Isles*, English Universities Press, 1971

Morgan, Paul (ed), *Inspections of churches and parsonage houses in the Diocese of Worcester*, Worcestershire Historical Society, 1986

Morris, John (ed), *Domesday Survey for Gloucestershire, Herefordshire and Worcestershire*, Phillimore, 1982-3

Nash, Russell Treadway, *Collections for a History of Worcestershire*, 1799

Noake, John, *The Rambler in Worcestershire*, Longman, 1854

Noake, John, *Worcestershire Relics*, Longman and Noake, 1877

Noake, John, *Worcestershire Nuggets*, Deighton, 1889

Pevsner, Nikolaus, *Worcestershire*, Penguin, 1977

Pitt, William, *A General View of the Agriculture of the County of Worcester* (for the Board of Agriculture), 1813

Rackham, Oliver, *The History of the Countryside*, Phoenix, 1997

Rackham, Oliver, *The Last Forest*, Phoenix, 1998

Restored Invalid, A, *The Metropolis of the Water Cure*, Simpkin, Marshall and Co., 1858

Richardson, John, *The Local Historian's Encyclopedia*, Historical Publications, 2003

Shirley, E.P., *Hanley and the House of Lechmere*, Pickering, 1883

Stanford, S.C., *The Malvern Hill Forts*, Malvern Hills Conservators, 1973

Smith, Brian S., *A History of Malvern*, Leicester University Press, 1964 and Alan Sutton and the Malvern Bookshop, 1978

Southall, Mary, *A Description of Malvern*, 1823

Stevens, William (printer), *The Leisure Hour*, London, 1856, 1862

Three Counties Agricultural Society (pub.), Official Catalogues, 1950, 1976, 1984

Toomey, James, P., *Records of Hanley Castle c.1147-1547*, Worcestershire Historical Society, 2001

Turberville, T.C., *Worcestershire in the 19th century*, Longman, Brown, Green and Longmans, 1852

Vince, Alan, *Medieval and post medieval ceramic Industry of the Malvern Region*, from *Pottery and early commerce: Characterisation and Trade* (ed. Peacock) Academic Press, 1977

Watkins, Alfred, *The Old Straight Track*, Methuen, 1925 and Abacus, 1974

Watkins, Morgan, G., Continuation of Duncumb's *Collections towards the History and Antiquities of the County of Hereford*, Jakeman & Carver, 1902

Willis Bund, J.W., *Inquisitiones Post Mortem for the County of Worcester 1242-1326*, Worcestershire Historical Society, 1894

Willis Bund, J.W., *Worcestershire County Records, Division I, Quarter Sessions Papers 1591-1643*, Worcestershire County Council, 1900

Willis Bund, J.W., *The Civil War in Worcestershire 1642-1646 and The Scotch Invasion of 1651*, 1905, reprinted by Alan Sutton, 1979

Willis Bund, J.W., and Page, William (eds), *Victoria History of the County of Worcester*, Constable and St Catherine Press, 1901-26

Worcestershire County Council, *Malvern Hills Area of Outstanding Natural Beauty, Woodland Management Guidelines* and other publicity material

Worcestershire Historical Society, *The Red Book of Worcester*

Worcestershire Historical Society, *Lay Subsidy Rolls*

Worcestershire Historical Society, *Bishops' Registers*

Wrightson, Keith, *English Society 1580-1680*, Hutchinson, 1982

Local newspapers

The Malvern Advertiser
The Malvern Gazette
The Malvern News

Catalogues

House and property sales in the early 20th century

Fictional

Grindrod, Charles, F., *The Shadow of the Ragged Stone*, Elkin Mathews 1887, 1909

Symonds, W.S., *Malvern Chase*, North, 1881

Symonds, W.S., *Hanley Castle*, North, 1883

Index